Helping the Bereaved

HELPING THE BEREAVED

Therapeutic Interventions for Children, Adolescents, and Adults

ALICIA SKINNER COOK

AND

DANIEL S. DWORKIN

BasicBooks
A Division of HarperCollins*Publishers*

Library of Congress Cataloging-in-Publication Data
Cook, Alicia Skinner.
    Helping the bereaved: therapeutic interventions for
children, adolescents, and adults/ Alicia Skinner Cook and
Daniel S. Dworkin.
        p.   cm.
    Includes bibliographical references and index.
    ISBN 0–465–02717–2
    1. Grief therapy.   I. Dworkin, Daniel S., 1948–   .
    II. Title
RC455.4.L67C65   1992
155.9'37—dc20   91–57905
                                                            CIP

For Allison

For Beanie and Lee

Contents

CONTENTS

Contents

Preface and Acknowledgments

THIS book was written to help mental health professionals gain the necessary knowledge and skills to work effectively with the bereaved, both individually and in groups. The practice of grief therapy is based on an in-depth understanding of the process of grieving and its manifestations, and like other specialized areas of therapy, it requires expertise in assessment, diagnosis, and intervention.

In this book we guide the practitioner through the assessment process and provide criteria for differential diagnosis. We also include examples of a wide range of therapeutic interventions that can be used with individual clients of various backgrounds and ages. Since grief therapy is frequently undertaken in a group as well as in an individual context, we have addressed concerns related to this approach and provided guidelines for effective group work with the bereaved.

Childhood, adolescence, and adulthood are distinct life stages that require somewhat different approaches to assessment and treatment; however, the therapeutic needs of younger grievers are often overlooked. In this book we not only provide numerous case examples of clients of different ages, but we include two chapters that discuss manifestations of grief in child and adolescent populations and examine the therapeutic interventions available.

Because many therapy books assume that clients will be from white, middle-class backgrounds, they present therapeutic approaches that may be appropriate for only a limited segment of bereaved clientele. Cultural differences create a dynamic that, while often disregarded, can nonetheless have a major impact on the process and outcome of therapy. With the increasing diversity of our population, it is imperative that therapists be attuned to the importance and implications of cultural differences, and so we devote a chapter to the varied ways in which grief therapy can be affected by cultural factors. One of our aims in writing this book was to share a broad-based perspective with our readers and prepare them to work with bereaved clients from a variety of backgrounds in a wide range of settings.

In the closing chapter, we ask readers to engage in important self-examination. This type of introspection on the part of the therapist facilitates effective helping and is an ongoing process. As one confronts new issues raised by clients during their grief work, new questions are also raised for the therapist. Paying attention to one's own responses promotes self-awareness and growth, both as a therapist and as a human being.

Writing a book is an arduous task that requires the contributions and support of many people. Two experts in the field, Kevin A. Oltjenbruns, of Colorado State University, and David Balk, of Kansas State University, reviewed early drafts and gave immensely valuable feedback. Dr. Oltjenbruns's attention to detail, both in substance and form, greatly enhanced the readability of the manuscript. Dr. Balk raised several conceptual issues that resulted in our rethinking, and consequently revising, some key sections. His questions and suggestions helped us put our ideas into sharper focus.

Our editor at Basic Books, Jo Ann Miller, guided us through the final stages of writing. We very much benefited from her keen intellect and her persistence. By sharing her expertise and experience, she has expanded our appreciation of the skills involved in professional publishing.

Acknowledgment must also be extended to those who have significantly affected our thinking and our approach to therapy. We want to thank Drs. Nancy Kerr, Jacqueline Davis, Jesse DeEsch, Don Tosh, Al Nissman, Andy Lester, and Frank Eliott. Finally, several others helped us in very important ways during the undertaking of this project. These people, who may be surprised to find themselves acknowledged, include Alice Lewis Brown, Jeff Brown, Graham Luckett, Rosemary Holland, Janet Pipal, Nancy Downing, and Susan Ihlenfeldt.

CHAPTER 1

Introduction to Grief Therapy

IN the 1970s when we started consulting, teaching, and doing clinical work in grief and bereavement, little information was available to guide the practitioner. During the intervening period, much has been written to advance our understanding of the bereavement process, but less work has been done specifically on therapeutic intervention with the bereaved. Few books to date have focused on the psychotherapeutic aspects of working with this population from a mental health perspective.

This book, based on twenty years of experience, was written to give guidance to mental health professionals working with the bereaved in a variety of settings. In it we discuss issues pertaining to diagnosis, assessment, and treatment in the context of grief and loss. We present individual and group approaches to intervention and offer practical suggestions for incorporating a variety of intervention strategies into therapy.

Because we believe that the practice of grief counseling and therapy should be based on sound therapeutic principles informed by experience, research, and theory, we have integrated information from these sources throughout this work.

Our Experience as Grief Therapists

Each professional's experience is limited by the type of clients and the variety of situations he or she has encountered. Our combined experience covers a wide age range (including young children, adolescents, and the elderly) and a variety of loss situations (suicide, AIDS and other diseases, homicide, large-scale disaster, accidents), as well as clinical work in hospices, hospitals, university counseling centers, elementary and secondary schools, and private practice. We have attempted to share our wide range of experience through the inclusion of numerous case examples of clients with whom we have been privileged to work.

Like that of many therapists, much of our work has focused on middle-class Caucasians. We have, however, actively sought cases that would involve us with diverse populations. One of us has spent considerable time on two other continents learning about similarities and differences in the ways various cultures respond to loss. As the population of the United States shifts toward greater ethnic diversity, mental health professionals will increasingly be involved with people whose backgrounds are different from their own. Throughout this book and in a separate chapter, we discuss culture as a critical component in therapy and provide examples of barriers to effective therapeutic intervention, emphasizing the use of culture as a resource rather than a factor to be overcome.

Integrating Research-Based Knowledge

We feel that therapists often fail to take advantage of information emerging from the efforts of researchers in the field of grief and loss. In this book we have, when possible, grounded our formulations of therapeutic work in findings from empirical studies. The research on recovery from bereavement has much to offer the practitioner, and we have attempted to translate these findings into meaningful practices and interventions that can be used by mental health professionals. Where the outcome studies and evaluations of specific techniques and approaches were limited, or where research was unavailable, we have relied on our clinical experience and extrapolated from research findings in related areas.

Our Theoretical Perspective

Therapists with a narrow theoretical perspective often find it challenging to work with grief issues. Although our own orientation tends to be psychodynamic, we also draw from existential, cognitive/behavioral, and family systems perspectives when conducting grief work. It is important to recognize that grief resolution is not an event but a process, and what is needed in terms of therapeutic interventions in earlier phases may be quite different from what is required in later ones.

We have found that the initial adjustment phase fits into an attachment paradigm. A love object has been lost, and the client is facing the permanency of that separation. Emotional catharsis is emphasized during this stage, as the therapist gives the client permission to grieve and supports the person in that process. This loss evokes emotional and physical responses, and effective coping requires coming to terms with the experience emotionally, cognitively, spiritually, and existentially. The degree to which this occurs will vary from person to person and will usually continue after therapy ends.

As therapy proceeds, the emphasis is more on gaining insight into the implications of the loss and ways in which past issues may be complicating adjustment. During this segment of therapy, past relationships and coping patterns may be examined, as well as feelings about living without the deceased. Much personal growth can occur during this period, in which persons consider many aspects of themselves, their relationships with others, and their future.

The final phases of therapy typically assume a different tone as the focus of intervention changes. Adjusting to a loss involves more than acceptance of the death and an examination of personal issues. It often involves behavior and lifestyle change and usually includes shifts in one's identity as new roles are assumed and old ones are left behind. For example, research has shown that, initially, widowed individuals need empathy and support, whereas later on they need assistance in reinvesting in normal activities (Walker, MacBride, and Vachon, 1977). This reinvestment, as addressed in therapy, may involve some career counseling for clients who have been full-time homemakers and are forced to reenter the work force due to loss of a spouse. It may also include examination of issues relating to dating and remarriage after many years of living with a partner.

Each person presents a unique set of adjustment issues. We advocate selecting therapeutic techniques based on pragmatic concerns and the presenting issues. We have found, however, that strict behavioral approaches are not appropriate in the initial work of grief therapy and can even be counterproductive if clients feel the depth of their experience has been disregarded. On the other hand, emotional catharsis and reflection are rarely sufficient to help the bereaved "pick up the pieces" and restructure their lives after a profound loss. Therapists who are familiar with a variety of theoretical perspectives and techniques will be better equipped to address the needs of the bereaved.

Tenets of our therapeutic approach

Following is a review of the basic tenets that further define our philosophy of counseling and therapy and our approach to grief work:

1. Bereavement is a normal, natural experience, albeit traumatic and emotionally disruptive.
2. Despite what much of the literature suggests, the response to loss is not a uniform phenomenon. As Wortman and Silver (1989) point out, some people follow a commonly understood pattern, some never show intense distress, and others continue in a state of high stress for a long time. "Recognition of this variability is crucial in order that those who experience loss are treated nonjudgmentally and with the respect, sensitivity, and compassion they deserve" (p. 355).
3. The experience of grief occurs in two realms simultaneously: the intrapsychic or individual level and the interpersonal and social level (the family system and the relationships therein are typically the context for grieving). Grief work requires attention to both.
4. Grief is experienced within a broad social context. The societal view and acceptance of death as well as its expectations of "appropriate grieving" will influence the experience of loss for those living within that society.

5. Assessment of a client's personality, coping style, support systems, and cultural background is important in designing appropriate therapeutic interventions.
6. Therapeutic techniques are the means of stimulating the client's coping skills. The choice and timing of a therapeutic intervention should be geared to the client's needs and goals, not dictated by a rigid predetermined treatment philosophy.
7. The role of the therapist includes that of educator, facilitator, supporter, and catalyst for the growth of healthy, effective coping.
8. The quality of the relationship between client and therapist is critical to the change process. The therapist serves as an anchor to reality for the bereaved who has lost his or her sense of psychological equilibrium. A therapeutic relationship can develop only if the client and therapist share mutual trust and respect.
9. Personal characteristics of the therapist will, to a significant degree, hinder or advance the therapeutic process, so the therapist's ongoing self-examination and attention to personal issues surrounding death and other types of loss is critical.

Grief, Broadly Defined

Whenever we lose an object to which we have a close emotional attachment, either something or someone, we grieve. This book deals with grief after death. It should be remembered, however, that the sense of loss felt after a divorce, loss of a body part, being laid off or fired from a job, deciding not to have children, retirement (depending upon the circumstances), and many other life transitions can also trigger a true form of the grief response. Thus, at least an occasional sense of loss is part of our "normal" lives (Bridges, 1980). The grief after a death may be one of the most intense, but these other losses are no less real and deserving of attention.

In fact, most psychotherapy can be conceptualized, in part, as grief work, since loss of hope in the future, identity, self-esteem, personal power, and relationships with others are common themes often dealt with in this context. Bourdon (1991) found that incest survivors reported suffering from chronic grief over their lost childhood innocence. We highlight the frequency of the grief response because, left unaddressed, it can become a constant source of stress that eventually can affect even our physical health (Osterweis, Solomon, and Green, 1984).

Basic concepts

As the field of grief counseling has developed, the need to differentiate among the terms once used interchangeably has become more important. This need has grown out of an increasing awareness and understanding of the complexity of the process. It is not simply an exercise in semantics, because the more sophisticated our understanding, the more effective the interventions we can design to further the healing process.

Bereavement is the general state of being that results from having experienced a significant loss. It is the most comprehensive descriptor for one who has experienced the death of a loved one because it encompasses a wide range of reactions—emotional, cognitive, spiritual, behavioral, and physical.

Grief refers to the intrapsychic process of regaining equilibrium after a loss and requires reorganization on both emotional and cognitive levels. The manifestations of this include emotional catharsis and obsessive thoughts of the deceased. However, the process of re-evaluating spiritual issues and the presence of physical symptoms and behavioral changes also indicate that this intrapsychic process is occurring.

Duration of the grief response is usually discussed in terms of what is normal (how long should the acute emotional, physical, and behavioral reactions last?). Although there is no definitive research to guide us on this subject, these acute symptoms are expected to diminish within six months to two years (Cook and Oltjenbruns, 1989). After particularly difficult losses however (like the loss of a child), intense grief is likely to persist past this period of time.

Mourning is the public expression or sharing of the feelings of grief. This usually takes the form of a ritual such as a funeral service or wearing black. The period of mourning can vary significantly by culture, and considerable variation is seen among individuals and families within the same culture.

Grief work is the process by which the bereaved comes to terms with the death of a loved one. It is difficult and takes a great deal of emotional and physical energy to restore a sense of balance to one's life. To a significant degree, it requires a new identity and sense of reality.

Anticipatory grief is an experience of grief that occurs prior to the death of a loved one and emanates from the expectation of emotional pain and the life changes the loss will bring. Although it does not completely prepare a survivor for the emotional experience of the actual loss, it does allow time for resolving emotional issues with the deceased and preparing for the future. Sudden death is particularly difficult to handle since it usually does not allow this process to take place.

Resolution of grief is the result of accepting the reality of the loss both cognitively and emotionally and reorganizing the many facets of one's life (personal identity, relationships with others, use of time, meaning of life) to accommodate the absence of the deceased. Thus, it is not a return to "one's old self," because the death of a loved one changes us and our world profoundly and permanently. Resolution is referred to as a "process" because the efforts to adjust never really end and require continuing energy, albeit to varying degrees. The evidence that the major phases of resolution have occurred include the ability to remember the deceased without the intense pain experienced after the death, together with renewed energy and enthusiasm for living and for other relationships (Worden, 1991). Wolfelt (1987a) has suggested that the term *reconciliation* is more appropriate to describe this phase of healing, given that we never fully resolve our pain but continue to adjust as time goes on.

Anniversary reaction is an increase in the intensity of the grief response at certain times even after there has been some resolution to the loss. Certain days or times of the year that have significance (for example, birthdays, holidays, seasons, the date of death) can trigger thoughts of the deceased, and some of the earlier pain may return for a short period of time. As long as this response subsides after the anniversary period, even if it occurs each year, it is a necessary step toward healing. If, on the other hand, an old wound is opened and the pain shows no evidence of ending, an important unresolved facet of grief may still exist and professional attention may be warranted.

Normal grief responses

The grief response is multifaceted and includes all aspects of one's being—emotional, cognitive, spiritual, behavioral, and physical—simultaneously, so a holistic approach is needed in order to fully accept and understand how pervasive the adjustment process can be. It is the experience of this holism, no doubt, that causes the sensation of being "out of control" during bereavement. Our entire organism is affected, as if a shock wave has jolted the system. The aftermath—that of accommodating to the external change(s) and our internal reactions—is manifested by grief symptoms.

The *emotional turmoil* grief engenders is like no other. The reactions can be intense, overwhelming, and out of conscious control. The bereaved may feel as if they will go on indefinitely. For many people, fear, loneliness, guilt, sadness, anxiety, and helplessness are just some of the feelings experienced. Clients need to be reminded that all emotions are legitimate and worthy of expression and should not be held to a standard of rationality. For example, one of our colleagues experienced a period of anger at his mother because she died just two days before the dissertation experiment he had planned for a year was to be run and thus had disrupted a critical schedule. This reaction was not logical, of course, in that his mother did not choose the time of her death. It did, however, make sense given our assertion that all types of feelings are possible and worthy of expression and resolution.

Feelings will change as the grief work progresses. They will ebb and flow like the tides of the ocean, coming and going, triggered by some event or experience or by nothing at all. The key for the bereaved is to express the feelings in whatever form is needed, to be assured of their normalcy, and to be given hope that they will subside over time.

The *cognitive changes* that occur can have the bereaved questioning his or her sanity. Difficulty in concentrating is common, as are disorientation, inability to make decisions, hallucinations of the deceased, obsessive thinking about the deceased, and, at times, thinking that the death never happened. For example, Yolanda used to receive a call from her mother every weekend for years before her death. Afterward, whenever the phone rang on the weekend, she would think instinctively that her mother was calling and then suddenly realize that this was not possible. In another case, one of our clients whose friend died had a dream in which she was communicating with the deceased and awoke when she felt someone touch her cheek. No one was in the room. She found this event comforting because she interpreted it as a sign that the deceased cared for her and was doing fine. Some clients report sensing the presence of the deceased in their home at night, causing a feeling of apprehension and even fear that the deceased has returned to harm them. These cognitive reactions will probably be short-term and not be indicative of pathology, but they need to be monitored with regard to how severely they are affecting the client's functioning.

Spiritual orientation concerns the meaning we ascribe to life and death, and plays a major role in how well we adjust to the death of a loved one. For some bereaved, loss intensifies their previous values. For others, the pain of grieving results in a major reassessment of prior beliefs, which contributes to their sense of confusion.

Behavioral changes evident of a grief response often include withdrawal from social relationships, a quick temper, crying, extreme dependence on others, loss of interest in activities, drastic changes in eating habits, and abuse of medication, alcohol, or other drugs.

The *physical manifestations* associated with grief run the gamut: tightness in the throat, shortness of breath, an empty feeling, problems sleeping, loss of energy, headaches, general pain, constipation. In fact, depending on the individual, almost any physical reaction is possible. The chronic stress caused by unresolved grief can also contribute to the development of medical problems such as ulcers, irritable bowel syndrome, and chronic pain.

Complicated or Pathological Grieving?

Since the realm of normal grief reactions covers a broad spectrum, from crying spells to hallucinations, the task of identifying when the healing process is proceeding normally and when it is not can be a difficult one.

In this book, we have used the term *complicated* rather than *pathological* to encompass the full spectrum of grieving styles and symptoms that indicate an impasse in the grieving process and possible detriment to the mourner, even though *pathological* has frequently been used in the grief and loss literature up to this time. Webster's dictionary defines *pathological* as relating to a "concern with diseases," that is, as an illness. But difficulties with the grieving process, which may require therapy, are not always a sign of a psychiatric illness such as depression or psychosis. It is inaccurate to label a client as pathological except where an identifiable constellation of psychiatric symptoms exists. Furthermore, this type of medical terminology implies an external etiology and a lack of personal efficacy regarding improvement, which is not helpful to the mourner.

On the other hand, the term *complicated* denotes a broader view. It implies that assessment regarding the degree of health is to be based on whether or not the tasks of grieving are occurring (that is, a developmental perspective). Within this framework, pathology or psychiatric illness is just one form of a complicated response that also includes avoidance of grief and chronic, delayed, and inhibited grief responses. (A complete discussion of these is presented in chapter 2.)

Counseling/Support Services Versus Grief Therapy

In the field of mental health treatment, the distinction between counseling/support services and therapy is often overlooked, and the two terms are used interchangeably. We believe that while there is much overlap of the two, they are not the same—either in what they offer clients or in the skills they require of the therapist. The ability to discriminate between the two has significant implications for initial treatment recommendations as well as subsequent interventions and therapist training. We will address these issues in detail in chapter 5; however, since a general overview of grief work is discussed in this chapter, it might be helpful to begin the discussion with a brief examination of some of the differences.

Counseling/support services. Counseling/support services target individuals going through an "uncomplicated" grief process, with no significant blocks to the tasks of bereavement. These people have successfully coped with severe stress in the past and, even though they may be experiencing some difficulty with the process, can be expected to work through the current crisis gradually even without professional help. Nevertheless, they can still benefit from education about the mourning process, problem solving around adjustment issues, help with the expression of emotional reactions, advice about their unique concerns, and guidance about decision making during this difficult time.

Dealing with these specific areas, along with caring, support, and a willingness to listen on the part of the counselor, group leader, or group members will keep the normal grieving process moving forward. This type of intervention in a group format (Compassionate Friends, bereavement support groups at Hospice, Widow to Widow, and the like) also acts as a preventive measure in that regular observation within a counseling/support setting increases the likelihood that difficulties that occur will be identified and addressed in some forum. Assistance like this can be provided by trained professionals, trained volunteers, or the members of self-help groups (Worden, 1991).

Grief therapy. While counseling/support services can be a helpful component of any treatment program, when complicated grieving occurs, an additional intervention—grief therapy—is needed. Complications usually indicate that (a) a client has personality, developmental, or emotional issues that have not been resolved prior to the current crisis and are surfacing at the present time; and/or (b) the circumstances of the loss are unusual (for example, AIDS, suicide, war-related death) and are creating a complex grief process. In the former case, we must identify and help resolve the underlying issue(s) as well as attend to grieving. Thus, psychotherapy is intertwined with grief work, resulting in an adjustment process that can be an arduous one.

Grief therapy implies the need for significant emotional and cognitive changes to occur within the client. To act as a catalyst for these changes, the therapist needs an in-depth understanding of (a) the psychology of human growth (how people normally develop cognitively and emotionally), (b) how people change, (c) what role a therapist plays in this process, (d) child and adult psychopathology, and (e) the therapist's own personal issues and how they might affect interaction with a client. In a counseling/support setting, where individuals are proceeding normally through the grief process and the goal is to maintain this momentum, expertise in the above areas is not as essential as it is in grief therapy.

Theoretical Explanations of the Pain of Loss

Although our attention in this book will be primarily on the applied aspects of grief work rather than on the theoretical underpinnings of such work, it is important to have a conceptual frame of reference as a guide to the proper treatment approach. Such a framework, by defining how the change process is perceived, provides a "cognitive map" that guides assessment and choice of interventions and provides benchmarks for monitoring and evaluating progress. The psychological systems that make grieving such a painful experience provide us with a means of conceptualizing and understanding the struggles we observe in the bereaved. Our purpose in this discussion is to provide an overview of issues in this arena.

Freud (1917) explored the grief response in *Mourning and Melancholia*, which was an attempt to differentiate between normal grief and depression. He felt that the primary work of grieving was for the bereaved to withdraw the energy (life force, libido, identity) that he or she shared with the deceased. He called the original process of connecting with this significant other *cathexis* and its outcome *identification* (that is, the sense that this person is part of one's identity or ego). The process of eventual separation, or *hypercathexis*, unfolds as the memories and feelings attached to the deceased are intensified or reexamined until they have become so vivid and firmly fixed internally that they feel real enough to provide a sense of permanent connection and security. At this point the bereaved is able to accept the ending of a physical connection with the deceased and form new attachments.

The object relations point of view espoused by Volkan (1981) expands Freud's theory. First, Volkan supports "identification" as a healthy coping mechanism in that aspects or qualities of the lost object (someone or something) are incorporated into one's already-existing personality. He points out, however, that an unhealthy response (termed *introjection*) sometimes occurs whereby the lost object is not assimilated but becomes just an addition to the already-existing personality. Thus, no integration takes place, keeping the bereaved from letting go and moving forward. This problem is often manifested in the long-term use of "linking objects," which take the place of the deceased and represent the split that is felt internally (Volkan, 1981). This is problematic because "only when the lost person (object) has been internalized and becomes part of the bereaved, a part which can be integrated with his (her) own personality and enriches it, is the mourning process complete. With this enriched personality the adjustment to a new life has to be made" (Pincus, 1984, p. 409).

Bowlby (1969, 1973, 1980) believes that one of the limitations of

Freud's theory was its complete focus on intrapsychic mechanisms, with no attention paid to the interactional factors of attachment and separation that pertain to reactions within the external environment. Bowlby does not believe that Freud's "identification" is the primary mechanism at work in grief. Rather, his "attachment theory" posits that infants are instinctively attached to their mothers out of a sense of survival. It is the breaking of this bond that stimulates the grief response in the infant. This attachment behavior continues into adulthood and is directed toward both persons and other systems such as religious groups, work groups, and political groups (Bowlby, 1969).

Bowlby suggests that the mourning process is similar to the separation anxiety felt by infants when they perceive mother is not there for them. Whenever we lose someone or something to whom we are emotionally attached, the childlike feelings of loss and fear for our survival resurface, and we search for a way to regain a sense of safety within the environment. Parkes (1972) supports Bowlby's view of grief resolution as attachment to new objects rather than settlement of old attachments.

Some question whether or not Bowlby's model, which has been generally accepted as the basis for understanding the grief response, fully addresses the extent of the disequilibrium felt by the bereaved. Bowlby rejected Freud's theory of "identification" and the concomitant object relations explanation, which some feel has limited our understanding of the grief phenomenon (Klass, 1987). We agree with this conclusion. Rather than being mutually exclusive, the concepts together provide a more complete context for bereavement than either one alone. Grief is both an intrapsychic and an environmental adjustment process, and interventions must take place in both arenas. Lindemann (1979) spoke of this when he asserted that the bereaved need to review their interaction and relationship with the deceased in order to know what to preserve and then apply that understanding to future relationships.

Busick (1989) has discussed a synthesis of two other theories that explain the pain, confusion, and growth potential within the grieving process. She begins with Dr. Carl Jung's construct of the psyche: a *conscious ego* which is our identity; a *personal conscious* which contains "shadow" aspects of ourselves that we do not know exist, or that we deny because they do not fit our identity; and the *collective unconscious* which, unlike the others, is based not on individual experience but on knowledge resulting from the evolutionary development of humans and includes concepts we all understand, such as that of the "hero." Campbell (1968, 1971) suggests that people maintain their conscious ego (identity) until a life crisis such as a death occurs. Then, because part of what has defined them—a relationship or role—is gone, they are forced to reassess their basic assumptions about who they are. As this struggle unfolds one gets in touch with archetypal images and intense emotions embedded in the "collective unconscious." For the bereaved the most important images are femininity and masculinity, the acceptance of which can provide new ways to answer the basic questions about life's meaning. The feminine aspect represents the natural balance within nature, that is, life and then death. Embracing this archetype means accepting that one will die but that life is meaningful anyway. The masculine aspect relates to our uniqueness as human beings, specifically our ability to be conscious of our actions and to control our environment to a significant degree. Coming to terms with the existence of these polar opposites and the emotions they engender creates an inner peace.

As Busick (1989) points out, for the bereaved this means that his or her identity loses one of its defining aspects upon the death of a loved one. The depth of the struggle to redefine oneself after this loss will be related to the degree of ego investment in the deceased. During this identity confusion the "shadow side" emerges, wanting to be included in the new identity. One task of growth and bereavement is to begin to acknowledge these qualities and incorporate them as useful aspects of one's personality, allowing, in turn, access to the emotions of the archetypal level and setting the stage for a struggle for acceptance of the feminine and masculine elements of existence. The outcome is a new sense of oneself and of the meaning of life, the elements of grief resolution. This entire process is not linear, of course, and is ongoing throughout a lifetime, but the "hero's journey," as Campbell (1968) has called it, is the path of coming to terms with some of the most basic realities of our existence.

Models of Grief Resolution

Early work in the area of bereavement conceptualized grief resolution as a series of stages. More recent work has focused on the tasks to be completed in order to effectively cope with loss.

Stages

Kübler-Ross (1969) stands out as one of the early leaders in the effort to understand the grief process. Her description of the experience of grieving grew out of her work with dying patients. However, Kübler-Ross's findings have been commonly referred to as stages and are often applied to those grieving the death of someone else. The five components, as they apply to bereavement, are discussed below.

1. *Denial:* Even if a death has been anticipated, a significant degree of numbness or shock is often experienced once the event actually occurs. The reality of death is so hard to comprehend and accept that it takes some time before it is more than solely a cognitive realization and becomes an emotional experience as well. During this transitional phase, it is common to scan the environment for any sights or sounds that indicate the deceased is still alive. This behavior over a prolonged period of time may be an indication of a "complicated" grief process.

2. *Bargaining:* Once we fully acknowledge the loss, there can still be a strong wish that, somehow, it is not permanent. We may engage in a dialogue with a "higher power" in order to make this happen, for instance, promising to live a more productive life if the deceased would only return. A response like this has a magical, childlike quality and often stems from an instinctual fear that we cannot go on without the deceased.

3. *Anger:* For the bereaved, expressing frustration with the inability to hold on to the deceased and the pain of the loss can take the form of anger directed at a "higher power," the deceased, oneself, physicians, or a variety of other targets. After a suicide or homicide, the focus of anger can also become the police, the legal system, the funeral home, or the insurance company representative, since the work of these professionals underscores the reality of the loss.

4. *Depression:* This stage has come to represent the sense of profound

sadness and emotional pain that bereaved people sometimes experience. However, to be precise, using the term in such a comprehensive way is inappropriate since clinical depression, when it occurs, is part of a complicated grief response and represents a severe reaction to loss with specific components. (The distinction between grief and depression is discussed in chapter 2.)

5. *Acceptance:* At this point, the bereaved has reorganized his or her loss into some acceptable framework and is able to reinvest energy in the present, be hopeful about the future, and retain memories of the deceased without prolonged intense pain.

There are several limitations to the use of Kübler-Ross's model. First, as already noted, her work was done primarily with dying patients. Applying her findings to bereavement, although certainly relevant, does not fully communicate the breadth of grief work. Second, many people have misinterpreted her stages as being absolute and linear. The potential danger is that the bereaved will compare their reactions to the "norms," and their spirit will be bolstered or diminished accordingly. Any rigid paradigm, of course, does not take into account characteristics such as gender, age, and culture. Kübler-Ross's work, however, has been a springboard to a more comprehensive description of bereavement.

Tasks

Worden (1982, 1991) has provided the framework used most recently in grief therapy. He describes a series of tasks, which provides us with guidelines for our approach to grief work. Worden suggests the following four tasks to achieve resolution:

1. To accept the reality of the loss
2. To experience the pain of grief
3. To adjust to an environment in which the deceased no longer exists
4. To withdraw emotional energy from the relationship with the deceased and reinvest in new relationships

The task model suggests that the healing process is a developmental sequence of activities, one building on the other. Yet it should be remembered that growth is never linear. The bereaved will cycle and recycle through the tasks, handling them differently at different times, and sometimes tackling more than one task at the same time.

We think that Worden (1982, 1991) has provided a useful and comprehensive framework for tracking the progress of the bereaved. Since his model is developmental in nature, it is consistent with our belief that grief is an ongoing process requiring varied interventions as individuals progress in their grief work.

Kübler-Ross's description, however, can be viewed as embedded in Worden's task model. Her denial phase is one of the elements of the first task of accepting the reality of the loss. Bargaining, anger, and depression are part of experiencing the pain of grief. In a limited way, Kübler-Ross's stage of acceptance can be used to summarize the last two of Worden's tasks.

Positive Outcomes of Bereavement

Death and the ensuing bereavement are natural parts of human existence, and as such, they each have both positive and negative aspects. In Western society we tend to focus almost exclusively on their painful elements, but their potential for having a positive impact on our lives is great indeed. The Chinese culture recognizes this balance in their symbol for crisis, which signifies both danger and opportunity.

Accepting the reality of death can remind us of the importance of the present and of our current relationships. Resolving grief can leave us stronger and more self-reliant yet more connected to others than before (Malinak, Hoyt, and Patterson, 1979). A sense that our existence is limited can motivate us to create meaning in our lives (Benoliel, 1985). And bereavement is an opportunity for families to grow closer together. In essence, we may be stimulated by the pain of loss to reassess our priorities, which can enhance our quality of life.

It usually does not help a client who is grieving to be told that there can be a positive outcome to the pain he or she is experiencing. But sooner or later, as part of the process of resolution, the bereaved must find some meaning in the experience and a reason to go on living. As the grief work unfolds, an exploration of whether or not positive elements exist can at least broaden the client's perspective as to the potential benefits embedded within the struggle (Oltjenbruns, 1991).

Specific Types of Loss: Therapeutic Issues

Each loss is a unique experience. It is influenced by a variety of factors, including the circumstances of the loss. As we write this book in the early 1990s, three causes of death are receiving increased public attention: AIDS, suicide, and war-related death. Given the harsh nature of AIDS and societal reactions to it, the grief of family members, lovers, and friends is a complex process needing special attention from therapists. In the United States and many other countries, the aftermath of suicide has become an all too common occurrence. It is not the grief itself but the nature and intensity of the response that makes suicide survivors unique. The Desert Storm confrontation in the Persian Gulf as well as more recent global conflicts continue to alert us to the trauma of war and the subsequent need to heal the psychological wounds we so long overlooked in our Vietnam War veterans.

Our goal is to provide an introduction to the unique aspects of these kinds of loss, as well as to discuss treatment implications. As previously mentioned, unusual deaths such as these may necessitate therapy in order to address fully the emotional consequences of the losses. Each of these tragedies (as well as many others) generally involves multiple loss issues and complex reactions.

AIDS

As the AIDS epidemic grows, we are gradually becoming aware of the needs of those people grieving a death to this disease. The focus to date, by the public and the helping professionals, has been on the reactions of the gay community. But the scope of this illness continues to widen. Of the 100,000 diagnosed cases of AIDS by mid-1989, 9 percent were adult women, most of whom contracted the disease through IV drug use or as the result of heterosexual contact (Centers for Disease Control, 1989). Of these, 72 percent were nonwhite and economically disadvantaged (Bell, 1989; Ybarra, 1991).

Concerns of the bereaved. Homosexual clients grieving the loss of a friend or partner as the result of AIDS present unique concerns as they work through bereavement. Because, in general, Western society does not sanction homosexual relationships, the grief experienced after a death is often not supported, recognized, or legitimized. This kind of "disenfranchised grief" (Doka, 1989) places a significant obstacle in the path toward resolution. Klein and Fletcher (1986) have identified other important issues as a result of their group work with those grieving the death of a person with AIDS. Some of the special concerns of this population needing exploration and resolution follow:

1. The surviving partner has fears of also contracting AIDS.
2. There is often guilt over one's possible role in having transmitted the disease.
3. As the partner approaches reintegrating into society without the deceased, social conduct must be reevaluated in light of the obvious physical danger.
4. The partner may have been the central focus of the survivor's life, and now that he or she is deceased, feelings of isolation and abandonment may be heightened because family and friends may have long ago disowned the bereaved.
5. Because of societal disapproval of gay relationships, getting support during bereavement from traditional sources such as colleagues at work may be difficult.
6. The gay partner may be barred from visiting the hospital because of homophobia on the part of the hospital staff or family. Thus, the benefits of anticipatory grief and psychological closure cannot be obtained. Surviving partners may even be excluded from the funeral, losing the needed opportunity to say a final good-bye.

Grieving the death of a person with AIDS is also difficult for heterosexual friends or family members, as we found in one of our treatment groups.

Mr. Anderson's son officially died of pneumonia, a complication caused by AIDS. Mr. Anderson had refrained from telling even his friends about the disease for fear of their harsh judgments of his son, whom he cherished. More difficult was the fact that he was a member of a church that did not sanction homosexuality. How would he explain this to the congregation? By the time he entered the group, his sense of isolation was intense. This was compounded by his feeling that not acknowledging the true circumstances of his son's death was somehow admitting that he too was rejecting his son. Yet his love for his son far outweighed any reservations he might have had about a homosexual lifestyle. Acknowledging to the group that his son had died from AIDS was a major step toward healing. With the members' support and acceptance of the circumstances, he was able to see that the way his son died was neither a negative reflection on himself nor a negation of the sensitivity with which his son engaged life. With the restraints removed, he was able to grieve naturally.

Helping a client acknowledge such a sensitive issue is important. For as Worden (1982) points out, the first task of mourning is to accept the death, including the circumstances of the loss. Mr. Anderson took many weeks before he was able to relate the full story of his son's death. He decided to risk being honest only after experiencing the group members and the leaders as consistently caring and nonjudgmental during the first four sessions.

Guidelines for intervention. The therapist's personal feelings about homosexuality and AIDS are key to the effectiveness of any intervention strategy. Remaining nonjudgmental when dealing with the bereaved is paramount considering the lack of societal support for their grief (Frierson, Lippmann, and Johnson, 1987). Since the client has often been the caregiver to the deceased, the normal pain of bereavement may be compounded by residual effects from this stressful role. There may be a need for an intense emotional catharsis, and the therapist must be prepared to support this phase of grief work. If social support has been cut off, which is often the case, finding a support group for the bereaved is crucial in the effort to reduce the sense of isolation (Greif and Porembski, 1988). Schoen and Schindelman (1989) also remind us that while the bereaved may be grieving one death, he or she may be facing other losses as well. This is especially true in the gay and lesbian population, which has been disproportionately affected by AIDS-related deaths. Thus, treatment might include exploration of anticipatory grief.

Suicide

The following section on grief in the aftermath of suicide is a composite of our own clinical experience as well as a review of much of the recent literature (Dunne, McIntosh, and Dunne-Maxim, 1987; Lukas and Seiden, 1987; Dunn and Morrish-Vidners, 1987; Rando, 1984).

As the field of suicidology has developed, so too have important insights into this population of the bereaved. Rather than using the term *suicide survivors*, which sounds as if it refers to individuals who have attempted but did not complete suicide, it may be more appropriate to think of the bereaved as a *suicide "survivor-victim."* This is an attempt to communicate that he or she is, to a significant degree, also a victim of the suicide. For each deceased, it has been generally estimated that there are, on average, five to seven such survivor-victims. Also, instead of describing a suicide as being "committed"—a verb that in Western society sometimes implies a criminal act—describing an individual as having "completed" a suicide lets us focus on the tragedy and not, even inadvertently, on passing judgment. Finally, note that suicide happens in all types of families. There is no composite of the "at risk" environment, and the variables that interface to trigger the act are also diverse.

Concerns of the bereaved

1. Psychological: Nothing communicates the mindset that the therapist will encounter when dealing with survivor-victims better than their own thoughts. Lukas and Seiden (1987) give some examples of these thoughts from their work and personal experience:

Her suicide cheated me out of time to say good-bye.

I had no chance to say I'm sorry.

I feel guilty about feeling relieved.

I'm afraid it will happen to others in our family.

Suicide is a public admission that my love for my child was not enough.

If we'd only done something different, she'd be alive today. What did we do wrong?

Your friends avoid you. No one calls. You're alone.

What do I tell my colleagues at work?

The bereaved will invariably experience a sense of helplessness and powerlessness over not having been able to prevent the death. There is not only a profound sense of rejection and lowered self-esteem, but also the perception that the deceased preferred death to life with the bereaved. The bereaved may attempt to regain some sense of control by trying to understand why the suicide occurred, for if a reason can be found, then the world feels safe, orderly, and predictable again. There may be guilt over failing to save the deceased, having misread warning signs, or—since the act was deliberate—having deserved this ultimate act of rejection. The bereaved may blame others (therapist, media, police) in an unconscious effort to assuage his or her own guilt or as a means of indirectly expressing anger regarding (1) the deceased, (2) the sense of rejection felt, (3) the disruption of family life, (4) the social stigma, or (5) others for not preventing the death. Anger is not usually directed at the deceased despite the presence of such feelings, which may be denied out of fear of their intensity or their unacceptability.

2. Social: Given that social support serves to facilitate the grief process, its absence, due to societal taboos against suicide, can complicate the process of healing. Society sometimes attaches a stigma to the bereaved, as if he or she might have caused the death, failed to prevent it, or might even do the same thing. This may cause the bereaved to voluntarily withdraw from the community. As in any period of bereavement, family communication can become disrupted, especially by scapegoating, in an effort to find an explanation for the event. There may also be unexpressed fears about who else in the family might attempt suicide. Friendships too can be strained, as friends sort out their own reactions before offering support.

3. Personal: In the aftermath of any death, the bereaved goes through a period of personal disorientation. In the case of a suicide, the adjustment can be particularly difficult and may include (1) learning to accept the limits of one's control over others; (2) dealing with the sense of betrayal, which can lead to a mistrust of one's own judgment or a desire not to get emotionally close to anyone in the future so as not to risk such pain again; and (3) the need to adjust to being in the "spotlight"

as the focus of police or insurance company attention. The degree of guilt that is often felt can be manifested in forms of self-punishment such as medical problems or self-abuse. Suicidal ideation can be a manifestation of the anger at the deceased turned toward the self or the need to be with the deceased.

Guidelines for intervention. To work through grief after a suicide is a difficult task and a slow, complex process. To "hang in there" with the client requires great patience and skill on the part of the therapist. Although our general guidelines for grief work discussed throughout this book apply to suicide survivor-victims, there are some specific suggestions we want to make here, given the unique aspects of this type of loss.

Therapists need to identify and work with the full range of the client's emotional reactions: (1) explore the sense of guilt and encourage the expression of anger (even if it is directed at you), and move past this to the hurt, pain, and fear that usually lie beneath; (2) if the suicide was an end to the deceased's suffering, the client may feel a sense of relief and needs to acknowledge and accept this reaction; (3) stimulate the expression and resolution of the client's sense of rejection; (4) be careful not to collude in scapegoating behavior, as it is the client's way to avoid dealing with his or her own feelings of sadness; and (5) understand the bereaved's need to search for a reason for the suicide but recognize that, in some cases, since only the deceased can know, the client must try to live without an explanation. Therapists will also need to foster the completion of unfinished business with the deceased, encourage the client to take advantage of support from others and not withdraw into isolation, and reinforce the client's need to mourn with meaningful death rituals.

War

Although casualties in the Gulf War were limited for the allied forces, the renewed occurrence of armed conflict reminded us that many therapists are working with and will continue to work with veterans and their families. As a result of war, clients may include family members left behind, military personnel who witnessed the death of their comrades, and those civilian groups living near the front lines both suffering the effects of being terrorized and grieving over the death of loved ones. Many individuals are still grappling with their losses incurred in previous conflicts, such as Vietnam.

While we can only introduce this topic here, it is our hope that we can stimulate a renewed dialogue about interventions that will benefit these groups. After highlighting some of the special aspects of this type of loss, we will discuss post-traumatic stress as it relates to the grief response to war-related death.

Concerns of the bereaved. There are many grief issues that are particularly relevant to the death of a loved one in a combat zone.

1. Unfinished business: Although there may be time to prepare for the separation from family when a soldier goes into combat, the pain of this separation may overshadow the need to resolve problematic interpersonal issues, and this "unfinished business" may surface later during the grief response.

2. Lack of preparation: The suddenness of a loss (for example, a call from a loved one after a recent bombing run, followed within days by notification of his death) heightens the degree of shock and denial experienced by the bereaved.

3. Anger: Anger may be directed at the loved one for putting himself or herself in harm's way, at the government for sending him or her into the war zone, at the "enemy," or at the injustice of losing a child, parent, spouse, or friend.

4. Preoccupation with the death: Given that death in combat is always of a violent nature, the bereaved may become preoccupied with the details of the death in an attempt to answer questions about the circumstances, which are often sketchy in the chaos of war. She or he may focus on the terror, helplessness, pain, or loneliness that the deceased might have felt.

5. Unresolved grief: As Worden (1982) has pointed out, the first task of grieving is to accept the reality of the loss. But what happens when a soldier is reported as missing in action? In this case there remains the hope that he or she will be found. How, then, does the bereaved know when to let go and grieve? The possibility of unresolvable grief increases with this type of ambiguous loss, and maintaining hope for a loved one's return is a complicating factor in deciding when to let go and fully grieve.

6. Social stigma: We learned from the Vietnam era that the circumstances of a war may influence how soldiers are perceived, thereby affecting positively or negatively how their death is viewed. During the Vietnam War the legitimacy of grieving became entangled with the stigma attached to the war. This reaction is similar in some ways to the stigma sometimes attached to suicide, which limits the amount of social support the bereaved may receive.

7. Reactions of the veteran: Post-Traumatic Stress Disorder (PTSD) is a delayed but persistent condition characterized by depression, guilt, and grief, as well as a reexperiencing of a trauma in the form of flashbacks or nightmares and intense anger, anxiety, and emotional detachment. It is the response to being exposed to a traumatic and unusual event (Silver and Iacono, 1984; American Psychiatric Association, 1987). A significant number of Vietnam veterans still suffer the aftereffects of their experience (Shehan, 1987), which was used to define this syndrome, sometimes called Delayed Stress Syndrome (DSS). And there are some researchers (Widdison and Salisbury, 1990) who believe that the core of this response is often unresolved grief.

> A significant aspect of the problems attributed to DSS are the result of grief-related reactions to significant losses which were repressed while in the service because American culture, coupled with military training, did not facilitate the expression of such emotions. It was not until the individual separated from the service and returned home that defense mechanisms could relax, allowing the emergence of the repressed grief. (p. 295)

Looking at PTSD/DSS as a form of grief reaction provides us with an overall framework for conceptualization, assessment, intervention, and monitoring progress with such clients. Rather than focusing treatment on a particular symptom, we can work toward resolving the tasks of grieving.

A number of grief responses are prominent in veterans and are part of PTSD/DSS. There is always a sense of sorrow over the death of fellow soldiers, but there can also be a feeling of guilt over having survived while others did not (*survivor guilt*), which can sometimes lead to overt or subtle self-destructive behavior upon returning home (threatening suicide or driving while intoxicated). A sense of loss may also be the result of feeling that one has abandoned friends left behind (Cook and Oltjenbruns, 1989). Finally, soldiers find that in combat they may have to behave in ways that do not fit into their identity or value system, and this triggers a grief response for the lost sense of self.

Guidelines for intervention. As in most cases of grief, support from those who have suffered a similar trauma can help to reduce the feeling of being alone and misunderstood, so group therapy can often be helpful to veterans (Figley and Salison, 1980). The tendency of some veterans to distance themselves from painful emotions that are part of the war trauma is contrary to what is actually needed if the veteran is to avoid severe emotional disorders (Tick, 1985). The therapist must accept the task of challenging the client to approach his or her feelings even though expressing them may be an intense and, at times, even overwhelming experience.

Although family relationships can be adversely affected, little attention has been given to addressing the family system issues that arise (Hogancamp and Figley, 1983). Couples work and family therapy, though beyond the scope of this book, can be useful approaches for helping the veteran reconnect with significant others, which is vital to healing. Moreover, it gives family members a chance to learn how to communicate in ways that encourage the grief process (how to be empathic and nonjudgmental, when to ask questions and when to accept silence). To a significant degree, healing requires that the bereaved recount the events of the trauma and receive acceptance and support. Meeting this need might be difficult for family members as they deal with their own shock when hearing about the horrors of war. Helping them handle their reactions so they can still reach out to the bereaved may also be part of their therapeutic work (Shehan, 1987).

These are just a few of the issues therapists may find themselves addressing with clients grieving as the result of war. It seems reasonable to suggest, therefore, that more professionals become well versed in this realm of intervention so that veterans of both the past and recent wars will receive the help they need.

CHAPTER 2

Individual Assessment: Clinical Considerations

B EFORE decisions can be made regarding therapeutic interventions, a comprehensive initial assessment should be conducted. This chapter explores the components of such an evaluation with the adult client. Although we will present a detailed framework as a guide, we are not implying that our framework should be used in exactly the same way with every client. Conducting an assessment with an openness and a willingness to be flexible and creative rather than adhering to a cook-book approach allows the therapist to continually achieve new insights, on both verbal and nonverbal levels, and to tailor the evaluation process to each client.

Although an effective treatment plan always begins with a thorough evaluation of the client's condition and needs, assessment is an ongoing process throughout treatment itself. The therapist must remain open to new data and the revision of previous conclusions, which may dictate a change in the course of therapy.

Therapist's Style

A great deal of information must be collected during an assessment, and though this may appear to be a difficult task, if appropriate questions are asked, a clear therapeutic direction will usually emerge. One challenge to the therapist is to determine, given the time available as well as client need, which topics can or must be covered during an evaluation session(s). Another is to avoid the trap of becoming so focused on data gathering and so structured in one's approach that the interview sounds like an interrogation and allows little room for therapist flexibility and spontaneity. Despite the need for data, caring and support must be the cornerstones of any assessment, and they can be communicated in many ways.

The pacing of the session is one method. For instance, it is best to move back and forth between a focus on content and on affect, thus communicating the importance of both aspects of the client's experience. Pausing occasionally during the interview to encourage the client to report on how she or he is feeling is an example of this. The degree of client participation in the interview can also communicate the therapist's respect for the bereaved (does the therapist limit the client to simply answering questions passively or is the bereaved invited to exercise some control over the session by expressing his or her reactions to how the session is going or by offering what the bereaved thinks is important information missed by the therapist?). Clients should be encouraged to express feelings about the tempo as you go along, or you might explain why you are conducting the session as you are and invite questions. In fact, it often helps clients to have a written outline or verbal explanation of what will occur in the intake or initial interview so that they are better prepared to participate.

Framework for Assessment

The overall goal of an assessment is to answer the questions, Who is this person (personality and coping style), what were the circumstances of the loss, and what type of intervention is needed to facilitate the grief process? To accomplish this, the therapist must gather information on two levels: the factual (Level I) and the metacommunicational (Level II). These can also be described as content and process. The first level of information gathering is direct and concrete; the second is more subtle, employing primarily nonverbal information. It pertains, for instance, to how the client expresses himself or herself behaviorally or in tone of voice, what the client does not say, and the therapist's gut reactions. (See table 2.1.)

The factual data of Level I, the first phase of evaluation, can be obtained during a face-to-face interview with the client or prior to the first session using an assessment questionnaire. However, the face-to-face interview has the additional benefit of allowing the therapist to gather the more subtle information of Level II through observation of the client's communication style and behavior during the evaluation.

One of the benefits of beginning an assessment by gathering factual information rather than just promoting catharsis is that clients can usually answer questions of this nature with some ease and clarity. Since recently bereaved people often cannot concentrate and make decisions easily, being able to accomplish this task can foster some sense of self-efficacy and a concomitant sense that they can make it through the crisis. If a client cannot participate even at this level because of low energy, depressed mood, or cognitive confusion, assessment may need to focus primarily on how to help that person cope with the next few hours and days. Intervention in these circumstances may include close supervision by family, the use of medication, or, in the most extreme cases of incapacitation, hospitalization.

TABLE 2.1

Assessment Framework

Levels of Assessment	Information Categories
Level I: Factual Data	Context of grieving Coping style Physical condition Support systems Spirituality and religion Cultural influences
Level II: Metacommunication	Nonverbal behavior Personal reactions of therapist

Assessment Level I: Factual Data

It is our experience that the bereaved come to a therapist when the circumstances of death were traumatic or unusual, the grief reactions are so overwhelming that psychological disorders develop, or the tasks of grieving are not taking place, resulting in chronic, delayed, or inhibited grief. In these cases an understanding of the difficulties and obstacles to healing comes from a careful survey of the circumstances of loss and the coping resources of the bereaved.

The first level of data to be obtained is primarily factual and involves six elements: (1) context of grieving, (2) coping style, (3) physical condition, (4) support systems, (5) spirituality and religion, and (6) cultural influences.

Context of grieving

The personal environment in which grieving takes place is the stage on which the bereaved plays out his or her unique experience of grief. This "context" is defined by the the client's expectations of the grief process and includes personal history, the circumstances of the loss, and the relationship with the deceased. Exploration of these issues provides a glimpse into the client's world and the opportunity to understand what perspective and sensitivities are brought to this life crisis. It also highlights avenues for therapeutic intervention.

What are the client's expectations? Since clients entering grief therapy seldom have information regarding the processes of grieving or therapy, the extent of their understanding should first be evaluated. They need to understand as early as possible what to expect in treatment so that they can be full partners with the therapist in the effort toward resolving their grief.

A by-product of this assessment and subsequent education is communicating to clients that they have an active role to play in regaining equilibrium. It can also provide a context for the intense feelings and reactions experienced, in effect, normalizing them and reducing the fear of "going crazy," as well as offering hope that the loss can be dealt with effectively. Clients should know that even though they feel "out of

control," the therapist has confidence in their ability to actively participate in the process of healing.

What were the circumstances of death?   To begin the evaluation, it is
helpful to allow the client to recount in detail the circumstances of the
loss. The therapeutic impact of listening with concern as the bereaved
tells his or her "story" cannot be overstated.

Understanding the circumstances of the loss can stimulate some
hypotheses about the likely course of the grief process. For example, if
the loss was anticipated, then the client probably had some time to
prepare. If the loss was sudden, then ambivalent feelings about the
relationship and thoughts left unspoken may become particularly problematic. If the way in which loss occurred is not sanctioned by society
(such as when a teenager causes an auto accident while intoxicated,
resulting in death), the bereaved may not feel free to grieve (at least
openly), may be embarrassed, or may feel condemned by society. The
type of loss and the unique reactions it may create have implications
for the approach to treatment in that it highlights some of the likely
obstacles to successful grief resolution (Raphael and Nunn, 1988).

What was the relationship with the deceased?   Understanding the quality
of the relationship between the deceased and the client is important. Not
only will it highlight some of the needs of the bereaved, but it can
provide insight into the personality and coping style of the client as
well. For example, a male spouse who has always felt in control of his
life may be wrestling with the sudden awareness that, ultimately, his
control is limited. If his marriage was an emotionally close and interde-
pendent relationship, he must now struggle with the experience of being
on his own and the awareness of his limitations. Alternatively, a female
spouse who has always been the dependent member of the couple may
now have to become more self-sufficient. In each case, a major identity
shift and lifestyle change will take place along with the grieving process,
which will need attention in therapy.

If the relationship with the deceased was conflictual, then, along with
the pain of loss, there may be a sense of relief that the stress of daily
living has been reduced. Unfinished business with the deceased complicates the normal grief process. Without resolving the conflictual feelings, it is hard to let go of the deceased and reconcile to the loss. Yet

the bereaved is left to do this on his or her own since the other principal party is no longer available. In such a case, the therapist needs to know the details of the interactions—the origin of the conflict, what form it took, the attempts at resolution, the client's role in it, and so on. Working this through will become a major therapeutic task.

What is the client's history of loss?   Previous losses and how they were handled can be good indicators as to how a client may handle the current loss. Exploration of the past sometimes reveals that there are parallel processes at work in the present. For instance, if there is unresolved grief from the past, a new loss may rekindle those old feelings. When this happens, it is unlikely that the current crisis can be resolved without attention to the historical situation as well. In fact, focusing solely on the current loss will probably lead to an unsatisfactory therapeutic outcome. The multiple levels of grieving taking place are dependent on each other; all need attention, as illustrated in this example.

> George is eighteen years old and has come in for therapy. He experienced the breakup of a romantic relationship six months earlier and cannot seem to deal with the loss. He has tried to get on with his life but the grief has not abated. As a personal history is obtained, the therapist finds that George's mother died ten years earlier. At that time the family had adopted the "keep busy" avoidance technique, so that George did not get the chance to deal with his grief. When his father remarried, George expected that he would once again have a stable caring family and not feel so alone. But his stepmother was emotionally unavailable to him, and he felt more alone than ever after the marriage.

The feelings of loss engendered by the ending of his romantic relationship have gotten George back in touch with the feelings of loss regarding his mother's death and his disappointment that the close family he wanted had not materialized.

Complexity of a different kind is found in this case:

> Sandy's demeanor in her first therapy session was that of uncontrollable crying. She had always been the "strong one" in the family, but

"suddenly" at the age of forty-three, she cannot regain her composure. Her parents were divorced when she was eleven years old. Within the last year, she has had a miscarriage, a close friend completed suicide, and Sandy's father had just been diagnosed with colon cancer. In addition to incessant crying, Sandy has an intense need to continually confront her husband about stopping his heavy smoking.

The multitude of current and potential losses, in addition to unresolved grief over the divorce, have taxed Sandy's coping system beyond its limits. This is sometimes called "bereavement overload" (Kastenbaum, 1969). She can no longer keep her emotions at a distance and is now faced with changing her long-standing identity as the "strong one" in order to fully grieve. While possibly useful in the short term, her efforts to regain some sense of control, by trying to keep her husband from getting sick, will prove to be inadequate in resolving her pain.

Are there secondary losses?   The bereaved may experience physical or symbolic losses that occur as a consequence of the death of their loved one (Rando, 1984). These secondary losses can sometimes be more difficult to deal with than the death itself. For parents, it may be the loss of their hopes and dreams for their child; a spouse may no longer receive social invitations since he or she is now single and no longer "fits in"; the bereaved may have to move from the family home because of the death; or the roles of family members may change. All of these are painful adjustments, yet many clients do not realize that they are legitimate losses in and of themselves and worthy of attention. They are often very relieved when the therapist points them out, validates their reactions, and assists them in coping with the changes.

Client's coping style

Laying a foundation for treatment decisions should be one of the goals of an evaluation. Knowledge of what attributes a client brings to the grief work helps the therapist determine strengths on which to build and areas needing assistance. Moreover, how crises have been dealt with in the past is a good barometer of what to expect in the present.

How has the client expressed emotional pain?   We can be fairly sure that, in some way, our client has been trying to cope with his or her loss. Asking a general question regarding the reactions to date, including inquiry as to the most difficult aspects of the grief experience, gives the client the opportunity to recount efforts to cope and the therapist the chance to fully understand the situation. This exercise is a projective device in that the bereaved will choose the most salient features of the experience, and thus begin to paint a self-portrait (that is, a glimpse of his or her value system, coping system, and the unique elements of the struggle). The therapist needs to follow up on aspects of the report that are unclear and on manifestations that are usually part of a grief experience but have not been reported.

It is important to highlight the successful coping mechanisms so that they can be reinforced, as well as to uncover counterproductive approaches (such as excessive medication, alcohol, or other drugs; denial of emotions; or bingeing as a way to "numb out"). Even though the major difficulties will usually be presented, the therapist should ask specifically about what the client sees as obstacles to resolution of grief work. Since these obstacles contribute to a sense of helplessness, identifying them and diminishing their control through short-term problem solving, or stimulating hope for finding solutions helps maintain the client's sense of self-efficacy.

Are there gender issues affecting the client's reactions?   Up until recently, the grief therapy population has been female primarily, with the consequent emphasis on women's issues in bereavement. While these issues need to remain salient, a new trend is taking place. The "men's movement," which has encouraged males to get in touch with and express their feelings, is bringing more men into general psychotherapy than before and is providing therapists with more opportunities to work with male clients who are grieving. Because this presents the therapist with the challenge of developing a sensitivity to the unique concerns of this population, we want to explore briefly some of these concerns as they relate to assessment.

There is little doubt that the expression of grief can be different for men than for women (Raphael, 1983; Lagrand, 1986; Parkes and Weiss, 1983; Oltjenbruns, 1989). Based on the work of Gilligan (1982), we can hypothesize that this may be due to early identity development. To establish their masculinity, boys must separate from the primary care-taker, typically their mother. In effect, the intimacy they experience with her becomes a threat to this identity. In a parallel way, future intimate relationships with women and men can be experienced as a threat resulting in a struggle to balance the need for autonomy with the wish to be emotionally close. Thus separation caused by death may put a male back in a familiar and sometimes comfortable place—an independent existence where the challenge to identity has been removed. The result may be that a male's experience of separation and loss may be less intense (but nonetheless difficult) than a female's, whose identity is more related to connectedness to others (Gilligan, 1982).

Along with individual developmental factors, Western societal norms and traditions make it difficult for many men to allow themselves to feel and express the emotionality or to accept the sense of feeling "out of control" that is often inherent in grieving. These reactions are often interpreted as a sign of weakness—as is the need to depend on others—which, during a time of bereavement, is often necessary. The male perspective on loss, in and of itself, may contribute to an inhibited style of grieving. Lagrand (1986) and Raphael (1983) both found that adolescent males tend to view loss as "a problem to be solved" rather than something to be experienced. Finally, in Western society men are taught to expend all their effort influencing their outer environment (achieving, competing, controlling) rather than withdrawing into themselves, which grieving may require.

It is with many of these influences and attitudes that men enter grief work. Which of these, if any, are operational will determine the therapeutic interventions chosen. To assess this we suggest evaluating the client's expectations of the grief process: what he hopes to accomplish and what he has done thus far. What were the norms in his family regarding emotional expression? How does he typically cope with stressful or emotional issues? Can he share his discomfort with family, friends, and colleagues? How does he assess his ability to cope with his loss thus far? And most important, why has the bereaved come for therapy?

The client's reason for coming in can tell you a lot about how to proceed. Although some men are aware of the pain of loss, others who have suffered a recent loss come to treatment for work-related difficulties, physical illness, stress, or a feeling of just not being themselves anymore. While they may recognize the importance of the loss, these other concerns are apparently more acceptable as a presenting issue.

As always, the assessment is geared to understanding what treatment approach will best fit the client. Some men may be ready for an intense, affective experience as they work through the pain of loss, whereas others are able to use cognitive/behavioral strategies to adapt, and although the emotional reactions are limited, they are sufficient for resolution.

We wish to share one word of caution. A therapist who insensitively challenges a client (male or female) to emote, or insinuates that the absence of affect is unacceptable, can become an obstacle to an adequate assessment. The therapist may do this in the belief that intense emotions are necessary for healthy grieving or under the assumption that lack of expression means the client is not being honest. In fact, expression of affect is not always a prerequisite for resolution of grief (Wortman and Silver, 1989). Clients who are not used to being emotionally expressive, while they might not admit it, can feel anger or fear at having their control challenged or a sense of failure at not meeting the obvious "standards" of the therapist. Although the therapist has the task of challenging each client to fully grieve, what form this grief will take is unique to each individual.

What is the client's developmental status?   The developmental stage of the griever is an important variable to consider when assessing a client (Cook and Oltjenbruns, 1989). Much of the bereavement literature has differentiated characteristics of adult grievers and child grievers (see chapter 3 for a discussion specific to the assessment of children), but as useful as this distinction is, it does not take into account the variation that is evident for each developmental stage within childhood or adulthood. This lack of differentiation ignores the abundance of available information on developmental changes in understanding death and its implications for the grief process.

Therapists need to refine their knowledge of developmental theory and research findings in order to perform a complete assessment. They should ask questions such as What is the child's understanding of death? When does a child acquire the concept of permanence related to death? How might loss disrupt developmental processes and what areas are most vulnerable at particular ages? A five-year-old will respond differently to a death than will an eleven-year-old; a thirteen-year-old will process a loss differently than will a nineteen-year-old. Grief reactions must be interpreted within the framework of cognitive and psychosocial development. Developmental stages provide the intrapsychic context of grief and limit or expand the processing of the experience.

Developmental issues continue to shift during the adult years, affecting certain aspects of grief. Elderly individuals cope with loss in a context that is very different from that of a young adult. For example, an elderly widow who experiences the death of her husband is also likely to be facing the prospect of her own mortality. Additionally, she may be experiencing poor health, reduced income, and restricted social roles. A young widow, on the other hand, may be dealing with the reality of single parenthood and having few role models her own age who have successfully coped with the loss of a husband.

Another aspect of developmental change that must not be overlooked relates to personal development. Some people have spent more time than others examining their place in the world and the meaning of their existence. Some will have developed philosophical attitudes and perspectives that allow them to integrate a loss more readily into their lives. Personal development also includes the development of ego maturity, and while those with mature egos still feel the pain of loss, they have a stronger sense of self and more personal resources from which to draw when dealing with this pain.

Is the client suicidal or homicidal? One of the most severe reactions to loss is a sense of hopelessness so extreme that suicide seems a viable alternative for ending the pain. In the first evaluation session, it is imperative to ask if the client has thought of harming himself or herself, or any other person. Note that the demeanor of the client is not the only indicator of lethality. Do not jump to the conclusion that the distraught client is at risk and the calmer client is doing well. In one case, we found that the client who was the most composed and articulate in our grief group eventually reported a history of suicide attempts, hopelessness, lack of self-esteem, and little self-efficacy—all risk factors.

It is a myth that asking about suicide will suggest this course of action to a client when it has not been previously considered. Since mild suicidal ideation is common in survivors, the opportunity to openly acknowledge such feelings can be a relief. The therapist can help the client understand what needs these feelings represent and explore healthy ways to deal with them. Suicidal intent can also take indirect forms such as not eating, taking extreme unnecessary risks, and refusing to deal with grieving tasks over an extended period. Since the meaning of a client's behavior cannot be assumed, the intent is worthy of exploration.

If suicidal intent is expressed, the therapist must evaluate its seriousness by finding out if a concrete plan exists, if the means are available, and if there have been previous suicidal thoughts, threats, or attempts. Is the client using drugs that might impair his or her impulse control? Is the client naturally impulsive? If these elements exist, the client may need to be hospitalized (either voluntarily or involuntarily) for observation and further evaluation.

Occasionally, the therapist may encounter a client who is acting out his or her grief by talking of homicide, a reaction that may indicate significant pathology requiring active intervention. The same information should be obtained as that from the suicidal client. If the therapist believes the threat is serious, both the police and possible victim(s) should be notified. Hospitalization is the option of choice for this type of client. It is also advisable to consult with a supervisor or colleague about the situation as soon as possible.

Physical condition

From the medical standpoint, mental health professionals should be reminded that the psychological reactions their clients experience may in fact be primarily caused by an organic condition (Hall, 1980), not by the loss itself. One cannot assume that the stimulus path is psychological to physical, even in grief work; sometimes a physical condition is causing or exacerbating an emotional reaction. If the physical condition is not evaluated properly, psychotherapy may be considered the most appropriate treatment, when actually medical intervention may be warranted, or a combination of the two.

From the psychological point of view, the therapist should not automatically consider a sudden change in the client's physical reactions (headaches, anxiety, pain, high blood pressure, loss of appetite) to be a sign that the grief work is not proceeding appropriately. Rather than an indication of an impasse to be resolved, physical symptoms can sometimes be a sign that a major emotional or cognitive shift is about to take place (that is, a new awareness). Often clients have been working up to this point for some time or trying to avoid it, at times unconsciously, because of the overwhelming feelings involved. As the psychological shift approaches, clients can react physiologically. For instance, some clients can accept their loss intellectually but not at a deep emotional level. As the reality of the loss penetrates to this depth, they may begin to experience intense anxiety. Once the breakthrough occurs, however, the anxiety usually abates along with the physical symptoms. Nevertheless, whenever physical problems develop, a medical consultation is warranted.

Are there physical problems indicative of poor coping? The client's history of physical problems and stress reactions are often a clue as to his or her ability to cope with emotional difficulties. Stress-related problems including certain types of ulcers, colitis, headaches, backaches, and irritable bowel syndrome can be used as diagnostic tools. A pattern of psychosomatic illness (often subconscious) may indicate a tendency to deny feelings (Pelletier, 1977; Lindemann, 1979; Justice, 1988). The therapist might need to challenge the client to bring the feelings into consciousness so that they can be resolved and the physical stress level reduced. The client should also be made aware that by focusing on the physical pain, he or she avoids unwanted but important feelings and thoughts.

Is the client under a physician's care? There are few individuals who can go through the grieving process without some physical manifestations of the struggle (often it is a severe drain on physiological resources), so it is always a good idea to have a client maintain contact with a physician as needed.

In the first assessment interview, ascertain if the client is already under the care of a physician and, if so, what type of treatment is underway. Occasionally, clients will have already begun taking medication, in which case, the therapist must find out what is being used and become knowledgeable about its positive and adverse effects, since it might affect the course of the grief experience. If, for example, a tranquilizer or antidepressant has been prescribed, it could inhibit emotional expression and slow cognitive functioning, thus interfering with the resolution of grief. Obtaining a release of information in order to confer with the physician and coordinate your efforts is highly recommended.

If medication is used at all, from the perspective of mental health treatment, it should be targeted to the specific need, be as low a dosage as possible, and be prescribed for a limited time only. For example, if insomnia is the primary problem, the client should receive a sleeping pill, not Valium or Librium, which are antianxiety agents (Pirodsky, 1981). They remain in the body far longer than the period needed to alleviate the insomnia and often leave the client feeling drowsy the next day. An effective sleeping pill will not have this side effect.

One of the hardest things for all of us to accept may be the degree of pain that is often part of the grieving process. Therapists understand that the only way to heal is to accept the pain and work at resolving it. Circumventing this work by the use of denial or medication, for instance, only prolongs the process. Yet we live in a society where anxiety is regarded as detrimental, and the desire is to "fix it" quickly. Although the therapist may feel the process is proceeding normally, family, friends, or the client may feel the need for medication because of the discomfort the client is experiencing. In this situation, it is best to encourage a medical consultation and to work closely with the physician.

Status of support systems

The existence of support systems and the ability of the bereaved to use them will greatly influence the grief process. Grieving is, to a significant degree, a lonely experience, but healing comes, in part, through reconnecting with the world. One way to reconnect is by sharing one's experience and receiving and accepting the caring of others. Limited social support during bereavement has been shown to be associated with high distress and poor outcomes as measured by physical and mental health. The appropriateness and benefit of support depends on the amount offered, the timing, the source, and other factors (Vachon and Stylianus, 1988). Identifying the resources available to the bereaved is part of a complete evaluation.

What role is the family playing?   Assessment of family norms and reactions to both the death and the client is essential. The environment within which the grieving takes place will either encourage healing or inhibit it. What are the family norms about grief? Is the family supporting in the grief process or presenting obstacles to resolution? Is the client allowed to talk and emote about the loss? The therapist needs to form an impression of the family interactional dynamics. Remember, however, that the grief process will be experienced somewhat differently by each family member.

Is there outside support?　Besides the family, support systems in general are an integral part of the personal environment. A healthy social community, separate from a dysfunctional family network, can sometimes offset the latter's negative effects. Does the client have close friends? How are they responding to the loss? Is the network being used effectively? Sometimes clients will report that their support system, despite the comfort it provides, is being taxed beyond its limit, that friends are feeling overburdened. In other instances, the client may be withholding from this support system in an effort to protect it and keep it intact. In both cases, a client can benefit from guidance regarding how to use the support of friends appropriately.

Spirituality and religion

Spiritual and religious beliefs can be of great comfort to the person who is grieving. By "spiritual" we mean the way one makes sense of life and death; "religion" can be the structure in which the bereaved may exercise his or her sense of this meaning. Exploring this realm helps the therapist understand how the client operates in the world, including the value system that he or she uses. It should also be remembered that the value systems of clients vary and might not fit into the above categories. In any case, a primary goal of the assessment is to learn about whatever personal philosophy is at work and how it is affecting the bereaved.

What are the client's spiritual or religious beliefs?　Spiritual and religious beliefs can help the mourner make some sense of the loss and provide the basis for meaningful rituals that assist in adapting to a new reality. The community of believers of which the mourner is a part can provide an understanding support system ready to help with the healing process.

41

At moments of extreme hopelessness (as when a person is suicidal), religious dictates that prohibit such action can stimulate a call for help.

On the other hand, there are clients who do not possess a clear spiritual or religious orientation that can be used to explain a significant loss. This is not always problematic, but some clients may feel overwhelmed trying to develop a philosophical or spiritual perspective while at the same time dealing with their grief.

How do the client's beliefs affect adjustment?   Although spiritual and religious beliefs are usually a comfort in times of grief, this is not necessarily the case. After a death, some clients stop going to church or synagogue altogether, claiming that their religion no longer provides satisfactory answers about life and death. If the deceased was a "good person," doing all the things the devotee is supposed to do, then it's hard to understand the cause of a painful or sudden death (Kushner, 1980).

If the death occurred in an unacceptable way, then religious principles might actually condemn the type of loss and create guilt in the bereaved. Given the stigma, the therapist may be the first person who is told about the actual circumstances of the loss.

Since the therapist will come into contact with a wide range of religious and philosophical attitudes, it behooves him or her to read extensively and have as much exposure to different perspectives as possible (Neuberger, 1987; Tigges and Marcil, 1988). This will help the therapist remain nonjudgmental and able to communicate in the language of the grieving individual. It is also important that therapists understand how their own spiritual and religious beliefs influence their therapeutic style.

Cultural influences

Increasingly, therapists are providing services to a culturally diverse clientele, yet many find themselves ill equipped to deal with their clients' needs and concerns. As the complex mental health needs of various groups begin to emerge, we are also becoming more aware of the influence of subcultures. Although our discussion focuses on ethnic differences, the reader should bear in mind that our statements regarding diversity can encompass regional and social class differences, groups affiliated with particular religious beliefs, and rural-urban distinctions as well. Any adequate assessment should include an examination of the influence of the systems of which that individual is a part. (In chapter 7 we present an in-depth discussion of cultural considerations in grief therapy.)

Many people identify with their cultural backgrounds during a life crisis more than at any other time. Given the stress of bereavement, even acculturated individuals look toward their ethnic roots as a means of maintaining continuity with the past. Immersion in prescribed rituals and support systems of one's culture can also help reduce the sense of loss and aloneness the individual is likely to be experiencing. Sometimes, however, an overidentification with a culture at the time of death can be unhealthy: a sudden adoption of cultural norms and customs not previously practiced may reflect attempts by the bereaved to "recapture" the deceased and keep parts of that individual alive through compulsively engaging in rituals that were important to that person. This is especially unhealthy if the values of the deceased were incongruent with those of the bereaved.

Assessing the cultural context of grief.   Guidelines for assessing cultural influences can best be put in the form of questions. By asking yourself the following questions as you work with individuals and families, you can maintain your sensitivity to cultural factors. You can also use these questions when working with other subcultures (not just ethnic groups) that are significantly different from your own in terms of values, beliefs, and traditions.

1. How strongly does the individual and family identify with their cultural group? To what extent have they assimilated into the mainstream of the country or community in which they reside? Is their ethnicity an important part of their identity? To what degree do they participate in their culture of origin?
2. Are cultural norms and expectations a source of conflict for the client? Are they interfering with the successful resolution of grief?
3. What strengths can you draw upon from the individual's cultural background that may be used effectively in the context of therapy?
4. Are there traditional customs and rituals that the person has not

been able to engage in because of the demands and expectations of his or her current living situation? Is this problematic for the individual?

5. Given the person's background and your own, what factors might potentially interfere with communication and understanding between you and the client?

6. What modifications or adaptations do you need to consider in your use of therapeutic techniques? Are some approaches inappropriate considering the cultural background (customs, norms, role relationships, mores) of the individual and family? What cultural considerations will affect your use of individual, group, or family therapy?

7. How can you most effectively incorporate the person's cultural beliefs, values, and traditions into the goals and process of therapy?

8. In what ways does your own cultural background affect your professional practice?

Assessment Level II: Metacommunication

The second level of assessment includes information learned through the process of interaction with the client and the therapist's ability to listen to metacommunication (that is, information beyond that which is communicated in words, such as nonverbal behavior, what is not said, the meaning of silence, and personal reactions of the therapist to the client).

Therapists are constantly bombarded with books and periodicals, new theories, and intellectual presentations regarding therapy. As a result, it is easy to forget that verbal and written communication are just two elements of the assessment arena with which we need to be concerned. We have, after all, been trained and encouraged to use many aspects of ourselves, not just our heads, in the treatment process—to listen with our "third ear" (Reik, 1946).

Level II requires the use of the "self" in the gathering of information (the therapist's feelings, thoughts, and reactions to the bereaved). It does not lend itself to a purely cognitive approach; it is a slow, intuitive process, fueled by data derived from an understanding of interpersonal dynamics and systems, good observation skills, and the knowledge of how the therapist's reactions to the client can be used in treatment planning. Therapists who have not yet focused on developing these skills, which provide the means for collecting much of the subtle but useful evaluation data, will need to do so if they are to help others do their grief work. Taking additional courses, attending experiential workshops, reading about therapy process, having close supervision of one's work, and personal therapy are just some methods of fine-tuning these skills.

Level II data are drawn from the experience of being with another human being. Periodically during sessions, the therapist has to put aside his or her intellectual skills and experience what it *feels* like to be with the client: what emotional or physical reactions to the client occur or what personal issues are triggered by the client's struggle. It helps to ponder these types of questions concerning interaction when working with the bereaved:

- What do I notice about this person?
- What is his demeanor?
- Did she walk into the room quickly or straggle in?
- Is he waiting for me to lead the conversation or does he take charge?
- Are her answers short and substantive or long and circular?
- Is eye contact poor? If so, what does this mean?
- Are emotions easily expressed?
- Are emotions overly expressed?
- What type of emotional response does this client elicit from me, and what does this tell me about him and myself?
- Do I like being with this client or not, and what does this tell me about myself and/or her?
- Given what I'm experiencing, how do I think others react to the client?
- How might the client handle the grief work I will encourage?
- How are my issues of grief and loss related to the client's?

Asking these questions is based on the premise that, even in the midst of the present trauma, many of the patterns of coping behavior that normally define clients in their daily lives will, to a significant degree, be exhibited within therapy sessions. These patterns reveal how the clients view the world and how they will cope with grief, and provide some of the data for designing therapeutic interventions.

Differentiating Complicated from Uncomplicated Grief

As we begin our discussion of complicated grief, note the importance of refraining from attaching a diagnostic label too quickly. One behavior or symptom is not enough on which to base diagnostic and treatment decisions. A comprehensive assessment over time is needed. While a complicated grief response is indicative of (but not limited to) "an interruption, absence or inhibition of mourning, i.e., lack of awareness, acknowledgment and sufficient expression of feelings" (Weizman, 1989, p. 15), note that a lack of the "sufficient expression of feelings" is not confirmed solely by the absence of intense emotional catharsis. Behavioral expression of feelings is also valid, as the following case illustrates:

> Jeff's father died of a sudden heart attack. They had planned to go to a World Series game together if the Brewers got there. The Brewers made it but his dad died just one month before the game. To express his sense of loss and respect for his father, Jeff went to the game as planned and decided to buy his father a souvenir, which Jeff, himself, could then keep as a reminder of his dad.

Signs of possible complicated grieving.   Several authors (Stearns, 1974; Gould, 1988; Burnell and Burnell, 1989; Jacobs, 1988) have identified "poor grieving responses" which might interfere with grief resolution. Table 2.2 lists categories of behaviors that might indicate problematic grieving and the need for therapy. They are based on the work of Demi and Miles (1987), which we have modified and refined, providing examples where appropriate.

Whether or not these factors indicate a complicated grief process will depend on their duration and intensity. There is no absolute time line for the grief period, although the most intense symptoms seem to abate within six months to two years, depending on the the individual and the circumstances of the loss (Cook and Oltjenbruns, 1989; Demi and Miles,

TABLE 2.2
Possible Warning Signs for Complicated Grieving

Avoidance of Grief

Mummification (the deceased's room is left unchanged long after the death)

Idealization (exaggerating the positive qualities of the deceased, which maintains a fixation on the magnitude of the loss)

Holding on to anger or guilt rather than saying good-bye and forgiving oneself and others

---

Chronic Grief (Also called Prolonged or Interminable)

Although loss occurred years ago, individual cannot speak of it without intense overwhelming pain

Years after the loss, unrelated events still trigger intense grief response

Themes of loss repeatedly come up in daily conversation

Years after the death, the bereaved has not resumed normal day-to-day functioning

---

Delayed Grief

A current loss or other significant event elicits exaggerated response, indicating unresolved loss from the past also exists

---

Inhibited Grief (Also called Masked or Repressed)

Neglect of health

Drug abuse, including alcohol and medication

Extended preoccupation with suicidal thoughts

Acting out (promiscuity, legal violations)

Persistent psychosomatic complaints, including chronic pain

Developing physical symptoms of deceased if he or she had been ill

Impulsive decision making (sudden radical changes in lifestyle)

Psychiatric Illness (May also be Masked Grief)

Psychiatric disorders (clinical depression, anxiety, brief psychosis, eating disorders, post-traumatic stress)

1987). If any of the behaviors and symptoms become incapacitating or do not diminish within the two-year period, therapeutic intervention may be necessary.

Clients at risk for complicated grieving. There are many predisposing factors that put an individual at risk for unresolved grieving. The following list includes those reported by Stearns (1984), Burnell and Burnell (1989), and Wolfelt (1988):

1. History of *family dysfunction*, resulting in a lack of coping skills and/or low self-esteem
2. *Inadequate support system* (friends, family, religious affiliation)
3. History of *multiple losses*, raising the possibility that some losses have not been fully resolved, thus complicating the current mourning process
4. Previous *psychiatric problems* (depression, psychosis)
5. Pattern of *psychosomatic illnesses*, indicating that the client has a habit of denying intense emotion, thus triggering intense physiological responses
6. A *"suffering life script,"* indicating that the client has little sense of self-efficacy and expects continual waves of misfortune in life
7. History of *drug abuse or addiction*, indicating a limited repertoire of coping behaviors and poor impulse control
8. Availability of social support for grieving is limited because of a *controversial type of loss* (abortion, AIDS, suicide)
9. *Ambiguous losses* such as a soldier missing in action or a kidnapped child in which there is uncertainty about return
10. Losses in which the *relationship with the deceased was problematic* (ambivalent, conflictual, dependent)
11. Situations in which maintaining an unhealthy response provides a *secondary gain* for a client whose needs can be met by not resolving the grief

Grief and Clinical Depression

Because they have many symptoms in common, an uncomplicated grief process can sometimes be mistaken for clinical depression. At other times a complicated grief reaction has actually developed into a true clinical depression. Distinguishing between these can be difficult, but success in doing so will dictate the direction and scope of the subsequent interventions (such as use and type of medication, type of psychotherapy, need for hospitalization). In this section we have provided some guidelines for differentiation.

Diagnosing depression using DSM-III-R

The *Diagnostic and Statistical Manual of Mental Disorders* (DSM-III-R) (American Psychiatric Association, 1987) reports that grief and depression have many symptoms in common. For example, both types of clients can experience despair, lack of interest in activity, hopelessness that the pain and emptiness will cease, suicidal ideation, guilt, and low energy. Recognizing that even uncomplicated grief can be severe, the DSM-III-R indicates that the diagnosis of uncomplicated bereavement is "not considered a mental disorder (that is, major depression) even when associated with the full depressive syndrome" (p. 222).

How, then, does one distinguish when the symptoms represent a normal reaction that will subside in due course, or when they denote a separate unique pathology? A further challenge is how to determine when both conditions exist simultaneously. DSM-III-R falls short of helping us answer these questions. The manual states that morbid preoccupation with worthlessness, marked functional impairment or psychomotor retardation, or prolonged duration suggests that bereavement is complicated by a major depression. Yet we have seen these reactions in both those grieving normally and those who are depressed.

Assessing depression versus grief

As Worden (1982) has pointed out, differentiating between grief and pathology "is more related to the intensity of a reaction or the duration of a reaction rather than the presence or absence of a specific behavior" (p. 58). With this and the findings of Robinson and Fleming (1989) in mind, we suggest four areas in which to look for data that distinguish appropriate grief from clinical depression:

1. Circumstances of loss
2. Personal context (characteristics and history of the mourner, including cultural background and family history)
3. Cognitive functioning
4. Intensity and duration of symptoms

Circumstances of loss. The type of loss can alert us to the possibility of a complicated or pathological reaction. If the loss was unusually traumatic, uncommon, or unexpected, we might expect the reaction to be severe, even in a client with a positive personal history. For example, after the suicide of a child, parents and friends may experience much guilt for not having "read the signs." Parents especially may feel as if they have failed in their duty to protect their child.

Personal context. In part, discrimination of the existence of clinical depression depends upon our assessment of how healthy the client was to begin with, as well as additional personality, cultural, and familial factors. It is into this "personal context" that we fit all the other information about the client and the loss. Thus, we start with a careful assessment. For example, if the client has a history of poor coping or previous mental illness, the odds increase that unresolved historical issues exist which might cause grief to deepen into significant depression or that depression may have existed prior to the grief response. In the latter case, resolving the current grief may still leave the underlying depression. Remember, though, that the cultural context will influence how we interpret the symptoms we observe.

Cognitive functioning. Freud (1917) felt that a negative sense of self differentiated the depressed person from the normal griever. In their review of the research directed at identifying the distinctions, Robinson and Fleming (1989) report that persistent, distorted, and negative perceptions of self, experience, and the future, along with guilt, self-blame, and hopelessness seem to be the primary differentiating factors between clinical depression and the depression-like quality of some grief reactions. This is consistent with the depressive schema, or negative triad, delineated by Beck, Rush, Shaw, and Emery (1979). In their cognitive therapy, depression is characterized by a negative sense of oneself, the world, and the future. The Beck Depression Inventory (Beck, Ward, Mendelson, Mock, and Erbaugh, 1961) has been used successfully to assess clients' cognitive coping style.

Intensity and duration of symptoms. Intensity and persistence of the client's reactions will have an impact on how the therapist views his or her condition. The significance of both must be interpreted in light of the client's personal context, the circumstances of the loss, and his or her cognitive coping style. Intensity and duration of symptoms cannot stand alone as measures of depression.

Intensity relates to the degree to which the client is affected by the loss—emotionally, cognitively, physically, behaviorally, and spiritually. In extreme cases, the client may be incapacitated, and medication or hospitalization might be required. Intensity alone, however, does not indicate clinical depression because, depending on the psychological makeup of the client, the intense symptoms might abate within a short time.

Duration of symptoms is a key factor in assessment, but how does one determine what is "too long"? The DSM-III-R states that "normal bereavement varies considerably among different cultural groups," which is certainly true but not much of a guide. It also states that the "reaction to loss may not be immediate, but rarely occurs after the first two or three months" (p. 362). (Our clients who did not fully grieve a loss until many years later would disagree with the latter.) This time limit does not seem appropriate to us either.

Table 2.3 provides some of the symptomatic differences that can be used to make a differential diagnosis. The first systematic attempt to do this was made by Schneider (1980). We have modified his original chart based on our own experience and in light of new information (Robinson and Fleming, 1989).

Even with these distinctions, differentiation between grief and clinical depression can still be difficult, as in the following example of a diagnostic dilemma:

Diane is twenty years old and the adult child of an alcoholic father who psychologically abused her, although she still felt emotionally close to him. He died in a hunting accident when she was nine years old. The result of the abuse and the sense of abandonment she felt after his death left Diane with low self-esteem and difficulty trusting others. Two months ago her mother died of cancer, and Diane is experiencing signs of severe clinical depression, including suicidal ideation and hopelessness.

Shall we conclude that such a severe reaction is appropriate and will subside in a reasonable time, given that Diane's mother was her only

TABLE 2.3
Differences Between Uncomplicated Grieving and Clinical Depression

	Uncomplicated Grieving	Clinical Depression
Loss	Recognizable, current	Often not recognizable
Reactions	Initially intense, then variable	Intense and persistent
Moods	Labile Acute, not prolonged Heightened when thinking of loss	Mood consistently low Prolonged Pervasive pattern
Behavior	Variable: shifts from sharing one's pain to being alone Responds to some invitations Variable restrictions of pleasure	Either completely withdrawn or fear of being alone No enthusiasm for activity Persistent restrictions of pleasure
Anger	Often expressed	Turned inward, not necessarily expressed
Sadness	Periodic weeping and/or crying	Little variability (inhibited or uncontrolled expression)
Cognitions	Preoccupied with loss Confusion	Preoccupied with self Worthlessness Negative sense of self and the future Self-blame Hopelessness
History	Little or no history of depression or other psychiatric illness	Probable history of depression, psychosis, or other psychiatric illness
Sleep Disorders	Periodic difficulties	Regular early-morning awakening
Imagery	Vivid dreams, capacity for imagery and fantasy	Imagery tends to be self-punitive
Responsiveness	Responds to warmth and assurance	Hopelessness and helplessness limit response

surviving parent? If so, then a diagnosis of uncomplicated grief is warranted. Or is it possible that the current grief reaction over her mother's death has also triggered an existing unresolved grief process, the combination of which is so overwhelming that a clinical depression has developed? We suggest that the two losses could be overlapping. First, there is grief over her mother's death, but it is too early to tell if this is a complicated process. Therapy needs to focus on both the recent loss and Diane's struggle (1) as the child of an alcoholic abusive parent and (2) with possible unresolved grief over her father's death. It may be difficult for her fully to resolve her grief over her mother's death unless resolution of older issues is achieved.

Diagnosing Bereavement Using DSM-III-R

For both assessment purposes and to satisfy insurance companies that pay treatment expenses, the therapist must contend with the issue of diagnosis using a formal classification system. Although some practitioners rebel at "labeling" a client, we believe that, beyond the insurance needs, and even though DSM-III-R is far from perfect, distinctions between grievers do exist, and diagnostic identification has important treatment implications.

The DSM-III-R is the standard diagnostic manual in the field of mental health and addresses the issue of loss in a variety of ways. The diagnoses that seem appropriate to the grief response are (1) Uncomplicated Bereavement, (2) Adjustment Disorder, (3) Major Depression, and (4) Post-Traumatic Stress Disorder.

Uncomplicated bereavement is the category reserved for the "normal" grief responses, which include a wide range of reactions. We presented a framework for distinguishing complicated from uncomplicated grief and *major depression* in chapter 1 and earlier in this chapter.

An *adjustment disorder* is defined as a maladaptive reaction to an identifiable and common stressor that occurs within three months after onset of the stressor and that has persisted for no longer than six months. It is assumed that there will be remission when a new level of adaptation has been achieved. This would seem to be a category for many of the complicated reactions we have described. Even though the loss may have occurred in the past (that is, more than three months ago), this diagnosis is often used because it is usually a recent stressor that acts as a catalyst to reawaken a grief process.

In situations where an event "outside the range of usual human experience" occurs, the intensity and scope of the grief reaction may be embedded in a *post-traumatic stress disorder*. This diagnosis can be used, for instance, in cases of a plane crash, a suicide, a murder, or where the death of others is witnessed.

Obstacles to Assessment and Diagnosis

Collecting appropriate information about the bereaved during the first interview and eventually formulating a diagnosis is a goal that can be difficult to achieve for a variety of reasons.

1. The client is emotionally distraught.
2. The client minimizes the extent of the grief response.
3. The therapist's issues inhibit the assessment process.
4. Grief over loss is not the presenting concern.
5. There is a limited treatment period due to financial restrictions.

Client is emotionally distraught

Clients often arrive at the first session in an emotionally volatile state, seemingly unable to focus on the assessment process. Given this kind of initial presentation, the therapist's tendency may be to stay on that affective level for much of this first interview. This can take the form of allowing the client to emote to the exclusion of data gathering, encouraging the repeated recounting of his or her story, or focusing on reflecting an understanding of the client's feelings and offering encouragement. Although these strategies have their place in the first session, without some limitation placed on their use, the therapist may leave that initial interview knowing very little of substance about the client (perhaps after having just put the person into a grief group!). The therapist was so busy being supportive that the primary assessment goal at this point—gathering data—was not accomplished.

It is difficult to gather data from an individual who is in great emotional pain, yet unless we do, a treatment plan cannot be developed. To this end, there is information that must be obtained in the first meeting: What is the client's physical condition? Is she or he suicidal or homicidal? Is there an adequate support system? Might crisis intervention be needed before treatment actually begins? Is there information that the client needs right away regarding the grief process? Is there one pressing issue that he or she needs to deal with immediately?

When the bereaved is emotionally distraught and the goal of the evaluation is not being accomplished, it is time to employ a crisis intervention strategy. The therapist needs to take control of the session and redirect the client to the factual areas requiring attention. This may be a more directive approach than many therapists take in actual treatment sessions. One must remember, however, that the goal of an assessment is to gather information and begin formulating a treatment plan—a very deliberate process. Of course, all assessment sessions combine emotional catharsis and data gathering. It is up to the therapist to strike a balance.

There are other benefits to this approach beyond gathering data. The client who is overwhelmed by his or her current emotions sees nothing beyond this pain. When therapists redirect their attention to other matters, it provides an opportunity to reactivate their intellectual capacities, thus creating some equilibrium and a pause from the sense of being out of control.

Client minimizes extent of grief response

As Wolfelt (1987b) has pointed out, often a client is aware of feelings of grief but minimizes them by not communicating the extent of his or her reaction, thereby giving the therapist the impression that everything is under control. As a result, the therapist might overlook common assessment questions by assuming the answers. The following case illustrates this type of situation:

Simone was a well-groomed, articulate, rather calm thirty-year-old woman who requested a therapy group because she was having great difficulty adjusting to the death of her brother, who had died from a rare blood disease. Given that her relationship with her father was very poor, her brother had been her primary male support. The therapist assumed from her demeanor and verbal presentation that she was uncomfortable but emotionally stable and needed to explore unresolved issues with her father as well as the current loss. Thus he did not ask about depression symptoms or lethality. Nor did he obtain a complete personal history. Once in the group, however, Simone reported being actively suicidal and having attempted suicide three times in the past. She also recounted a history of abuse by various men in her life.

Therapist's issues

Sometimes it is the therapist who gets in the way of an adequate assessment. For instance, if little information was gathered during an evaluation session, the therapist may report that "the client was too upset to participate in the process." While this is certainly true occasionally, we may want to look elsewhere for the difficulty. One possibility is that as a result of an intense empathic response, the therapist may have become so emotionally involved that it was hard to maintain the role of "observer" (that is, making conscious decisions when to attend to the affective domain and when to gather data). The result then is an interview centered on the affective realm only and controlled by the client.

Interestingly, sometimes the decision regarding what the bereaved can handle within a session is never even discussed with him or her. The therapist makes the decision without consultation, assuming what is possible, given the client's demeanor. But we don't really know what a client can handle unless we ask. It is surprising how much strength even a distraught client can access when appropriately challenged by the therapist. Proceeding on the basis of assumptions often means that the therapist is reacting to something within rather than to signals from the client; thus a countertransference reaction may be occurring wherein the therapist's own personal conflicts, history, and stressors impair his or her ability to respond to the bereaved (Teyber, 1988; Fromm-Reichmann, 1950). Warning signs of this problem include a therapist's intense need to be liked; assuming responsibility for causing or alleviating the client's pain; his or her own family norms limiting emotional expression, which can make working with a client's feelings difficult; choosing therapeutic interventions based on what he or she would prefer if in a similar situation instead of what the client actually needs.

To take charge of a session in the manner suggested, the therapist must have a plan of action and confidence in it and in himself or herself. This is most difficult for professionals early in their careers because they do not yet have the experience on which to base their judgment. Understandable as this may be, inexperience is no excuse for lacking a conceptual framework to guide the therapist's behavior.

Grief over loss is not the presenting concern

It is common for clients to present with issues other than grief (for example, depression or anxiety), even though grief issues may be significant. They may not report grief as the major concern because the feelings are outside of their awareness: the death may have occurred long ago and memories have faded, or they were told by significant others to "just go on with your life." Children may present with behavior problems that are actually a symptom of unresolved grief rather than the core issue needing attention (Lesee, 1983). Presenting a concern other than grief indicates either a conscious defense against unwanted feelings or clients' inability to acknowledge, possibly even to themselves, what is truly felt. A therapist's initiation of discussion regarding possible loss issues can give a client permission to recapture or uncover and explore feelings and reactions. No matter what the presenting problem, a thorough assessment should include a question about whether or not the client has had previous major losses.

Limited treatment period

The days of managed health care have arrived; consequently, there is a press toward time-limited therapy, accountability to third-party payers in the form of session-limit authorization, and substantial written summaries of treatment. In some cases, there is a three-session treatment limit for mental health issues, allowing time for crisis intervention only. Given the time factor, one might conclude that treatment must start immediately upon referral, and that time for extensive assessment is a luxury. We think this conclusion is a mistake.

First, we must not overlook the therapeutic effects of the assessment interviews themselves. Having a caring person to listen to them can help many clients feel less alone with their pain and more hopeful about themselves and the future. More important, gathering the appropriate information and thus being able to create a proper treatment plan will enable the healing process to proceed at its optimum pace. Without an adequate evaluation, the treatment program designed might be useless or harmful.

Bereavement Scales and Inventories

We have devoted this chapter primarily to the interactive process of assessment, but a variety of formal instruments that measure aspects of grief are also available. Gabriel and Kirschling (1989) have reviewed nine of these, including the Grief Experience Inventory (Sanders, Mauger, and Strong, 1985) and the Texas Revised Inventory of Grief (Faschingbauer, Zisook, and DeVaul, 1987). Other noteworthy instruments are the Grief Experience Questionnaire (Barrett and Scott, 1989), the Hogan Sibling Inventory of Bereavement (Hogan, 1988), and the Perinatal Grief Scale (Potvin, Lasker, and Toedter, 1989). Although most of these measurement tools are not currently recommended for clinical use, practitioners may want to explore their application in clinical research as they examine trends observed among their bereaved clients.

CHAPTER 3

Bereaved Children and Adolescents: Assessment and Diagnosis

MANY people assume that children are not capable of experiencing true grief; as a result, their reactions to death are not often fully explored and evaluated. Children most definitely do grieve, but their ways of expressing it are different from those of adults (Cook and Oltjenbruns, 1989; Salladay and Royal, 1981). They feel the same range of emotions as adults, but these feelings may not be obvious to the observer. Although children's experience of bereavement is painful and ongoing, their sadness does not seem to be as all-consuming as it is for adults. They can be laughing and playing normally one minute, and crying and needing comfort the next. Adults often misinterpret this shifting in attention and the accompanying emotions as an incapacity to feel the loss deeply. Accounts of adults who have suffered bereavement during childhood discount this interpretation. These individuals often have vivid images and strong memories of how they felt and how others responded to them during this time.

The features of childhood bereavement can be strikingly diverse. Regressive behaviors such as thumb-sucking and bed-wetting are common among younger children. Associated with this may be anxiety and fear about separation from other loved ones, resulting in clinging and dependency behaviors. Anger may be expressed through temper tantrums, aggressive behavior, discipline problems, deviance, or negativism

(Vida and Grizenko, 1989). Grieving children may also experience physical problems such as persistent insomnia, frequent nightmares, headaches, or loss of appetite (Koocher, 1983). Problems in school may emerge as well. Bereaved children, for example, may have difficulty concentrating, which will affect their academic performance; or their grief-related behavior (irritability, excessive withdrawal, decreased interest in play or recreational activities) may have an adverse affect on their relationships with classmates and teachers.

Like children, adolescents also respond in unique ways. Following the death of a loved one, adolescents may show intense emotional reactions, including confusion, depression, anger, and guilt; and these symptoms can continue over a considerable period of time. In addition, physical complaints and difficulties with eating and sleeping are also reported more frequently among bereaved adolescents than among nonbereaved peers (Balk, 1991). If unable to express their grief in acceptable ways, teenagers will at times "act out their grief" by engaging in antisocial behaviors (Cook and Oltjenbruns, 1989).

Many adolescents try to hide their inner feelings of hurt and pain in an effort to appear "grown-up." Since adolescence is characterized by increased independence, expanding physical strength and skill, and greater self-reliance, experiencing a loss (and subsequently grief) at this time is at odds with their normal developmental experiences. The following poem, written by a fourteen-year-old shortly after his sister's death, reflects this tension between "feeling strong" and looking toward the future versus the pain of loss, need for support, and longing for the past.

I am big and fast.
I wonder about the past.
I hear a calf crying for its mother.
I see tall pine trees.
I want to sail the seas.
I am big and fast.

I pretend I am an astronaut.
I feel like a big white blot.
I touch a soft leaf.
I worry about my mom.

I cry about my sister.
I am big and fast.

I understand my sister's dead.
I say no to drugs.
I dream about baseball.
I try to make good grades.
I hope to go to Auburn.
I am big and fast.

At times, adolescents may refuse to allow themselves the support of others because they want to demonstrate their control or because of fear they will be perceived as abnormal or different. What others think, especially peers, is extremely important at this age.

Hogan (1987) has indicated that sometimes adolescents adopt the role of "family savior" in order to prevent their families from disintegrating in the wake of a death. This may take the form of the "family clown," the one who makes everyone laugh and reduces the family's tension. Adopting this role means masking feelings of grief. Families might misinterpret the child's actions and think that he or she has not felt the loss deeply or that the child is coping well and rapidly resolving the loss.

Grief in response to a loss during one's youth may continue in varying levels of intensity for years. Although we know less about the reaction of adolescents to a friend's death than other types of loss, it is clear that grief in these circumstances has been underestimated (Balk, 1991). The following poem written by a twenty-two-year-old to his deceased childhood friend, Eric, gives testimony to the strength of early friendship bonds. He had carried Eric's tattered picture with him in his wallet for years until it was stolen. The poem was written shortly after this occurred.

Eric,

The fog seems to grow thicker
With every passing moment.
I close my eyes and smell the ocean
And hear the waves roll onto the beach
With a gentle crash.

The scene appears peaceful, but I can't shake
The feeling there is something out there.
A creature hiding in the fog.
I feel as though I'm in the middle of
A horror movie.

We loved a good scary movie, didn't we?

My good friend, I hear your calls.
I sit alone in the dark,
Hearing you, feeling you, being you.
My entire soul is yearning to see you, talk to you,
Touch you.

I feel a burden that you require something of me,
To achieve the dreams and goals you once had.
So many questions I long to ask.
So many wonderful things I wish to share with you.
Life.

Psycho was our favorite, remember?

The fog hides our faces from one another
But I know you are with me.
I tell myself you left me for a reason.
Oh, it still feels unfair.
Why did you go so soon, I never said good-bye.

Why . . . ?

Rob Lundsgaard

Special Considerations in Assessing Children and Adolescents

Much of the information presented in chapter 2 on assessment pertains to children and adolescents as well as adults. There are several aspects of assessing younger clients, however, that merit separate discussion: (1) therapists need to assess the child's or adolescent's opportunities to participate in grief-related rituals and ask questions about the death; (2) therapists may have to use nonverbal means to obtain the child's perspective; (3) parents and teachers should be seen as valuable sources of information about young clients; and (4) gestures of suicide among children and adolescents may take unique forms, so traditional means of assessing lethality may not be appropriate.

Involvement in rituals

An assessment should include a determination of involvement in the postdeath rituals (attending the funeral, for example), especially if the child did not have the opportunity to say good-bye to the deceased. In an effort to protect their children, parents often send them to stay with neighbors or friends and do not allow them to participate in the events surrounding the death. As a consequence, children have little opportunity to share their grief or to experience the loss as a member of the family. Lack of parental attention to the child's feelings of grief can have destructive effects on the child's sense of support and subsequent grief resolution. If these opportunities were missed, they may need to be recaptured in therapy.

Although adolescents tend to take a more active role in funerals, memorial services, and the like, than do children, they too may have limited opportunities in this regard. Deaths that occur at a geographical distance or relationships whose importance to the bereaved are not recognized by others (the death of a girlfriend or a favorite teacher) are examples of situations that may preclude involvement of bereaved adolescents.

Children and adolescents should never be forced to attend a funeral or view the deceased, however, since this may result in negative memories as well as anger toward the adults involved. Younger members of a family should always be given the option to participate and be fully prepared for what they will see. Therapists' questions about their participation should include probes that elicit information about these aspects of the experience.

Unresolved questions

Even if they were given the opportunity to participate in family events and rituals, children and adolescents may still have unanswered questions which disturb them. Consider the following examples:

Jeanne's mother was in a bus accident and was killed instantly. Her third-grade classmates at school told her they heard that her mother's head was cut off and that it rolled down a hill. The casket was closed at the funeral, and Jeanne had no information to indicate that this in fact did not occur. Weeks after the funeral, she had continuing nightmares stemming from this rumor, which was embellished at each telling. She eventually told her therapist this horror story, and was able to be reassured that her mother died of internal injuries and that her mother's head was still intact as she remembered it.

Three-year-old Timmy was very pleased that his parents were going to take him to Grandpa Joe's funeral. The night before the funeral, the "nice funeral man" showed him his grandfather in the casket and answered his questions very calmly and patiently. After pausing for a few minutes, Timmy looked worried and asked, "Why doesn't Papa Joe have any legs?" The funeral director assured him that he did and lifted up the bottom portion of the casket to show him.

Ian had been drinking with his seventeen-year-old friend just before the friend left in his car with some other members of the football team. They had a head-on collision with an elderly couple a few hours later. Many rumors were floating around school about the accident, in which five people were killed, including Ian's friend. Ian wondered whose fault it was, who was driving, and if alcohol had contributed to the accident. He felt extreme guilt but was afraid to talk to anyone who could provide some answers for fear that he would be blamed.

An assessment of children and adolescents should include the following queries: Did he or she have a chance to ask questions about the loss? Were these questions answered in terms that were understandable to the child or adolescent? The truth is usually far less painful, if conveyed in a sensitive and age-appropriate manner, than what young people can and do create in their own fantasies. Adults should not overwhelm children with more information than they can handle, but they should provide some facts, using the youngsters' own questions as a guide.

Use of Nonverbal Communication

Children, especially young ones, have limited verbal skills and often do not have the vocabulary or experience to describe accurately what they are feeling and thinking. They can also tire quickly during an initial evaluation session that consists mainly of questions and answers, becoming easily distracted and eager for the session to end.

One way to avoid losing the child's attention during the assessment period and ensure that a comprehensive assessment is completed is through the use of nonverbal methods such as drawing. Children's artwork can sometimes speak more clearly than do words, and they provide poignant examples of the unique viewpoints of children.

Mollie was eleven years old when her parents were involved in a motorcycle accident while riding up a canyon road. Her mother died instantly and her father was hospitalized for several weeks with serious injuries. At the time, she had a nine-year-old sister and a four-year-old brother. Her father brought her in to therapy approximately three months after the death, concerned because she was not talking much about the loss and she was having problems in school.

Figure 3.1 shows the picture that Mollie drew when asked to draw a picture of her family. When the therapist observed, "I notice that they don't have faces," Mollie replied, "That's because they don't know how they're supposed to feel." When asked why she did not draw herself in the picture, she answered, "Because I can't figure out where to put myself." It became apparent from the discussion that ensued that Mollie was feeling the void left in the parenting role by her mother's death as well as a great deal of ambiguity about her own role in the family. On one hand, she wanted to remain a child and feel protected; on the other, she thought that the family needed a "mother" and she was feeling responsible for the welfare of her younger brother, whom she described as "wild and out of control."

Figures 3.2 and 3.3 show the progressive changes in her family drawings over time. The symbol for her mother expanded from a simple cross over her father to a more elaborate version that included more positive elements (a heart and a rainbow). The series also shows changes in the perception of her little brother. In the first drawing, she

FIGURE 3.1

portrayed her brother's hands as tightly clenched and turned inward toward himself (perhaps indicating his inability to be comforted at this time), whereas in the second and third pictures, they became progressively more relaxed and expansive. The third picture showed more elements of home and family symbols (the inclusion of the cat and dog) as the family began to reorganize and regain their identity as a family unit.

Mollie still did not include herself in her drawings until several

FIGURE 3.2

months of therapy, when she spontaneously drew a picture that included all family members, with facial expressions for each one (see figure 3.4). Both the father and brother are smiling, while Mollie and her sister have smiles on one side of their faces. Her addition of the smiley-face on her sister's T-shirt suggests that she is clearer in her perception of the feelings of other family members than she is of her own. She has placed herself in the picture in the role of the oldest child, perhaps as an indication of giving up the maternal role and feeling more comfortable with her father's ability to parent her little brother. Most striking is the absence of any representation of her mother in the family portrait, suggesting an integration of the loss.

Mollie reached this stage after a series of individual and family therapy sessions in which she expressed her fears and concerns, was reassured by her father that he was able to continue to care for his family in the absence of their mother, and was given permission to express her grief with her father and receive comfort from him. These events took place after the father had recovered from his physical

FIGURE 3.3

injuries and from his own initial emotional shock at having lost his wife.

As this example illustrates, children's artwork can provide direction for a therapist's initial and ongoing assessment. Through the child's creative expression, therapists can identify areas requiring additional probing. This case also shows the importance of using a family approach when working with children following bereavement.

Some guidelines for using drawings as assessment tools include the following:

1. Provide simple instructions that are nondirective ("Draw me a picture of your family").
2. When the child has completed the drawing, ask about it with an open-ended question ("Tell me about your drawing").

FIGURE 3.4

3. If there are specific elements in the drawing that you would like to know more about, use questioning techniques or offer observations to elicit more explanation from the child. An example of this sort of probing can be found in the previous case study.

4. Never make evaluative judgments of the child's drawings such as "What a nice hat!" or "I really like your use of color." Such comments can influence the content and style of the drawings as the child attempts to please the therapist, thus inhibiting expression of true feelings.

5. Provide a variety of materials for the child to choose from (pencils, colored markers, plain paper, colored paper) so that your interpretation of the artwork does not reflect your inventory of art supplies rather than the child's psychological reality.

6. Consider a variety of elements when attempting to give meaning to the child's drawings: the presence or absence of color, facial expressions, body postures, proximity of the figures, inclusion or exclusion of central characters, omission of body parts, location of family members in relationship to each other, relative size of figures, and placement on the page.

7. Use art in a variety of ways; for example, ask the child to draw a sequence of family portraits showing the family before the death, on the day of the funeral, and in the present.

Parents and Teachers as Additional Resources

Adults serve as the primary source of information about themselves during a clinical interview, but children are often unable to supply all the relevant information needed by the therapist to do a complete assessment. While the self-report of children and adolescents is critical to any assessment—no one can tell you what they are thinking and feeling better than they can—there are other sources of valuable information that should be used when assessing younger clients. Two additional sources we recommend are parents and teachers.

Parents.   Parents can provide a psychosocial and developmental history on the child or adolescent, as well as indicate current levels of functioning at home, at school, and with peers and siblings. The parents' perception of the child and his or her position in the family are also important, since these will influence the child's behavior and thus the course of treatment. Also, caregiver involvement from the beginning of therapy will greatly enhance clinical work when significant others are seen as an important part of the treatment team.

Teachers.   Children and adolescents spend a large portion of their day with teachers and classmates. They may also behave quite differently in the context of the classroom than at home. Teachers are therefore in a position to offer some unique perspectives on the child and his or her adjustment, and because of their background and training, they may have special insights. Whenever possible, their input should be sought during the assessment stage. The reader is reminded, however, that parental permission must be obtained before contacting school personnel. Occasionally, this request is met with strong resistance, but in most cases, parents welcome involvement of additional professionals. School records can also be helpful, especially when there have been previously documented psychological evaluations or contacts with school psychologists, social workers, or counselors. Following a review of the records, these professionals should also be consulted, as should any therapists outside the school system whom the child has previously seen.

Assessing Lethality

Lethality is as much of a concern for therapists working with bereaved children and adolescents as it is for those working with bereaved adults. The escalating rate of suicide among adolescents is of major national concern. Suicides for this population have risen steadily since the 1960s, and there is evidence that suicide among children aged five to fourteen is a growing phenomenon as well. Although completed suicides among this latter age group are still relatively rare, suicidal gestures are not. Several studies have found that between 10 and 33 percent of children from clinical samples have contemplated, threatened, or actually attempted suicide (Stillion, McDowell, and May, 1989).

Youngsters of different ages react differently as they feel the anguish, emptiness, and sense of hopelessness that often accompanies the acute pain following a loss. For some, it can prompt thoughts of suicide. Therapists must be attuned to childhood and adolescent expressions of suicidal ideation and intent, and the various forms it may take. Whereas adults may overtly question the value of living, with such reflective statements as, "I'm not sure I want to go on living," or "What's the point in going on?," adolescents are more likely to express their self-destructive feelings through acting out (engaging in risk-taking behaviors, using alcohol or other drugs). Younger children typically experience much confusion about the event itself and the myriad of emotions they are experiencing. Preschool children, in an attempt to understand the death, may react to it through role playing. Some suicides have resulted from children using similar objects as those involved in the actual death (guns, ropes, pills) to "play dead." While these occurrences are usually accidental, with no intent to actually kill oneself, some very young children have verbalized "wanting to be with Mommy" to their therapists prior to these events. Obviously, parents need to be educated on recognizing clues to suicidal behavior in their children. They also should be reminded to be especially watchful of their children during the period of acute grief. This can be difficult for parents when they too are going through their own grief process, and other family members and friends may be needed to provide the extra caregiving and support needed by their child.

When suicide does occur, it may be precipitated by the loss but it is also often associated with previous suicide attempts, adjustment difficulties, and family problems. We want to emphasize, however, that this is not always the case, and the potential of suicide risk must be assessed and continually monitored in *all* clients.

Diagnosis Using DSM-III-R

The material presented in chapter 2 regarding adult diagnoses also applies to children and adolescents. In situations involving bereavement, the following diagnoses are usually the most appropriate, regardless of age: (1) Uncomplicated Bereavement, (2) Adjustment Disorder, (3) Major Depression, and (4) Post-Traumatic Stress Disorder. There are, however, some special considerations when assessing uncomplicated bereavement and major depression in children.

The DSM-III-R description of uncomplicated bereavement has been criticized for not including the range of childhood symptoms that are reported in the professional literature. Vida and Grizenko (1989) argue that the diagnostic criteria for this category need to be expanded to include features of childhood grief, or possibly a separate childhood bereavement category should be established. We also agree with their charge that the boundaries between uncomplicated bereavement, major depression, and adjustment disorder are not precisely defined for younger age groups.

Although major depression may be difficult to diagnose in younger age groups, we urge you not to overlook the possibility of this disorder occurring in the children that you see. While clinical depression is less prevalent in children than in adults, this disorder has been underestimated in children until the past few years (Rutter, Izard, and Read, 1986). Adolescents seem to fit the adult patterns of symptomology for depression, but depressed children often show unique symptoms not listed in the DSM-III-R criteria (Rapoport and Ismond, 1990).

If a child that you see is referred for nongrief-related issues but your assessment reveals a significant loss in the child's background, the client may still not fit the criteria for the four diagnoses most frequently used for the bereaved. These children and adolescents may, however, meet the criteria for various other disorders: Overanxious Disorder, Separation-Anxiety Disorder, Eating Disorder, or Conduct Disorder, depending on the symptoms displayed. Losses in early life can result in any of these disorders and residual grief issues should be addressed in therapy.

In situations in which the child has no diagnosed mental disorder and family issues appear to be the primary issue, we recommend the use of V Codes (conditions not attributable to a mental disorder) for either parent-child problems or other specified family circumstances. All too often children are the focus of treatment when in fact a family issue is involved. (Family therapists have long argued that psychiatric diagnosis must move beyond its focus on the individual client.) Dysfunction in families can frequently lead to the child becoming "the identified patient" and artificially labeled. Since no standardized and reliable format for diagnosing families is available at the present time, diagnoses are made with reference to individual clients only (Rapoport and Ismond, 1990).

CHAPTER 4

Processes of Change: Therapeutic Techniques

WHEN we are training therapists to work in the area of grief and loss, we are frequently asked, "But what does one actually do in the sessions beyond listening and reflecting?" Although this question stems mainly from the anxiety of inexperience, we also encounter more advanced therapists who have difficulty applying their knowledge of general psychotherapeutic skills and techniques to the specific area of grief therapy. In this chapter, we have selected a few therapeutic techniques from the wide range available to illustrate how they apply to situations involving grief and loss. Some are specific to grief and loss therapy, others have more general application, but all of them can be adapted for use with different age levels. Special intervention strategies for work with children and adolescents are also included in chapter 6.

Techniques are tools for facilitating the process of growth, change, and healing—nothing more, nothing less. They are only as effective as the therapist who is using them. In all cases, techniques should be selected based on the needs and attributes of the client and preferences of the therapist. Not all techniques work with all clients, and not all therapists use each technique with equal effectiveness. Techniques stimulate the *process* of therapeutic change; they do not replace it.

We encourage you to enlarge your repertoire of therapeutic techniques and explore their applications to bereavement. As we have discussed in chapter 1, different periods in the recovery process may require a different focus in therapy. We also urge you not to forget that the most basic skills of a therapist are oftentimes the most helpful. Sophisticated or interesting techniques alone cannot replace the need for active listening, appropriate reflection, and empathic responses.

The techniques presented in this chapter are organized according to their primary purpose and can be grouped into the following three categories: (1) techniques that promote an understanding and acceptance of grief reactions, (2) techniques that assist the client in exploring and expanding the legacy of the deceased, and (3) techniques that help externalize grief through symbolic acts. Each section concludes with an illustrative case study.

Promoting Understanding and Acceptance of Grief

Grief is unfamiliar to many people, and the first time it is experienced following a significant loss, it can elicit fear and uncertainty. Many feel that their reactions are "abnormal" in some way. Techniques that educate and inform the client about normal grief reactions can be reassuring and instill hope for recovery. It is also helpful for clients to realize that the grief reactions of others are legitimate even though different from their own, helping them to understand variations within their own family or circle of friends. Altered perceptions and insights gained in therapy can serve as a foundation for the work that follows. Several therapeutic techniques actively use these processes to encourage a healthy outcome for the bereaved. The two examples that we will discuss are bibliotherapy and reframing.

Bibliotherapy

Bibliotherapy is the therapeutic use of literature (Rubin, 1978). Through bibliotherapy, clients are often able to identify with the characters or situations they are reading about, which can lead to catharsis and insight about their own particular circumstances. Reading can also provide comfort, guidance, and information to the bereaved. Clients are given encouragement that others have survived similar losses, and their own feelings are validated as they read detailed accounts of recovery following bereavement.

Background.   Hynes and Hynes-Berry (1986) differentiate between interactive bibliotherapy and self-help bibliotherapy. Interactive bibliotherapy uses literature to bring about a therapeutic interaction between participant (client) and facilitator (therapist). In this approach, the therapist plays an active role in using the literary material as a catalyst for therapeutic change. In self-help bibliotherapy, the therapist may suggest specific reading for the client, but the client's response to it is not the focus of their sessions together.

Suggested guidelines.   It is very common for the bereaved (especially highly educated people) to request suggested reading matter. Usually the question is asked in general terms, but sometimes the clients have a specific area they want to explore. For example, a young widow may want information on how to help her children adjust. It is important for the therapist to be familiar with a range of books dealing with different topics related to death, dying, and bereavement. A wide variety of excellent literature is now available to help the bereaved, but the therapist should not restrict his or her recommendation to nonfiction; fictional accounts of families affected by grief (such as *Ordinary People*) can also be beneficial, as can plays and poetry. We recently came across a book of poems written by a mother after the death of her newborn son (Fritsch, 1988). Every other page included photographs of sculptures through which she expressed her feelings of profound emptiness and loss. In using this book with clients, we found that those who have suffered similar losses immediately connected with the images and narrative, commenting "She has been where I am now."

Although some therapists have one or two favorite books they recommend to almost all their bereaved clients, we suggest that all therapists familiarize themselves with a broad range of materials, because what works for one person may not work for another. Also, the educational level of clients, their age (child, adolescent, or adult), and their unique circumstances need to be taken into consideration. Some therapists have their own library of books they let clients borrow; others ask local bookstores to keep certain volumes in stock, or make sure they are available in an accessible library. Finally, therapists should know where to locate materials for visually impaired or non-English-speaking populations if they are likely to be working with these groups.

We have found many books to be helpful to our clients, including the following: *The Courage to Grieve* (Tatelbaum, 1980) is an excellent general discussion of the grief response and the healing process. *How to Survive the Loss of a Love* (Colgrove, Bloomfield, and McWilliams, 1983) deals with loss in all its forms. It includes poetry that reflects the grief experience and offers practical suggestions for surviving the emotional pain. Eda LeShan's book entitled *Learning to Say Good-by* (1988), originally written for children dealing with the death of a parent, has proven to be useful for adults as well. Widows will find that *Being a Widow* (Caine, 1988) accurately presents the issues unique to widowhood from the perspective of the author's personal experience of loss. Lukas and Seiden (1987) explore the aftermath of suicide in *Silent Grief.* This book is unique in that it is a collaboration between a psychologist and a survivor-victim. For clients whose loss is particularly incomprehensible (such as the death of a child in a car accident), the question of *why* is often the most persistent; *When Bad Things Happen to Good People* (Kushner, 1981) may provide some comfort for them.

Rodney, a bright twenty-six-year-old, came to therapy after the death of his father by suicide. He had many questions concerning the *whys* of suicidal behavior and its aftermath. "How could he take own life?" "Did he not care about me?" "Why do I feel like I did something wrong?" "Will I ever get over it?" Although these questions were explored in depth in therapy, Rodney found additional comfort in reading first-person accounts written by other survivor-victims of suicide. He also discovered that his feelings of intense guilt and anger were normal reactions, commonly experienced by others.

Reframing

Reframing is a technique the therapist can use to offer an alternative interpretation of a behavior or an event related to the loss. It challenges the individual's or family's perception and redefines the behavior or event (Minuchin, 1974).

Background. The concept of reframing is based on the assumption that we never deal with reality per se but rather with our perceptions and interpretations of a situation. As Watzlawick, Weakland, and Fisch (1974) have noted, our perception of our situation is not a simple matter of what is "out there." It is rather very much a function of how we define and make sense of what occurs. There are many different versions of "the truth," and some are more constructive and therapeutic than others. People experiencing intense grief often feel that they do not have a grasp on reality and need help in sorting out their experience of loss and the altered family dynamics resulting from it. This process permits the individual to gain a new perspective on the possibilities for positive adjustment and change. In order to perceive a different reality, the client's frame of reference must be substituted with one that fits equally well or better. Therapeutic reframing presents behavior or events in more positive terms that will be more conducive to therapeutic change. Helping the client to attend to his or her strengths and to develop the ability to see things in perspective reduces anxiety and uncertainty.

Suggested guidelines. It should be emphasized that reframing is not simply offering a Pollyannaish interpretation of a tragic situation. In fact, platitudes and clichés are usually met with resentment on the part of the client and are counterproductive since they indicate a lack of understanding of the depth of the experience. Reframing by the therapist, as the ramifications of the loss are explored, helps the client avoid tunnel vision and maintain flexibility of thought. Rather than simply presenting the reframing to the client, we suggest using questioning techniques in order to encourage the client's active involvement and collaboration in exploring alternative explanations and interpretations.

Wachtel and Wachtel (1986) recommend using reframing in a way that communicates an empathic appreciation of the client's experience. While the client's interpretations need to be heard and accepted, examining possible positive connotations of problematic behaviors and reactions can also be productive. This different way of looking at a situation can help individuals in a family to respond to each other in more constructive ways.

The Wallaces came to therapy eight months after their son had been murdered. Mr. Wallace appeared very controlled during the first few sessions and expressed little emotion. Often when speaking of her son and the means of his death, Mrs. Wallace would sob, but her husband made no effort, either verbally or physically, to comfort her. These behaviors were symptomatic of the dynamics between the couple that had been present since their son's homicide, and the emotional distance that had widened between them. Mrs. Wallace interpreted her husband's behavior as not caring about her or their son. In individual sessions with the therapist, she often said, "I don't understand why he doesn't miss him." After several sessions, the therapist said to the husband, "Sometimes emotional pain hurts so much that we don't know how to express it, and we just cut ourselves off from our emotions as a way of surviving. I wonder if this applies to you in any way." In response to this comment, tears started rolling down his face but he quickly regained composure. By introducing this alternative interpretation, it gave Mrs. Wallace a different way of looking at her husband's behavior (thus altering her own response to him), and it gave an opening to Mr. Wallace to begin expressing his pain at whatever level he felt comfortable.

Another family issue came to light when the sixteen-year-old daughter, Sarah, came in for a session. The Wallaces had been complaining that Sarah had become openly defiant, staying out past her curfew and, on occasion, coming home intoxicated. Mrs. Wallace remarked, "I don't know why she wants to cause us more pain. Doesn't she know what her father and I have been through?" In working with the family, the therapist pointed out that Sarah had lost her only brother and that she was probably dealing with her grief in the only way she knew how. She also suggested that acting out may be Sarah's way of trying to get her parents' attention, since her mother's intense grieving and her father's emotional distance had left Sarah to deal with her grief on her own. As the discussion progressed, Mr. Wallace revealed that he had felt very guilty about his son's death. He added that he did not feel worthy as a husband and father and thus was unsure what he had to offer his wife and remaining child. In the course of therapy, Mrs. Wallace and Sarah were able to share with him how much they did in fact need him, and how much they missed his characteristic tenderness and propensity to show affection. Also, the parents began to take more responsibility for parenting Sarah rather than ignoring her, and she was able to see that her mother's deep grief over her brother did not mean that she did not value her remaining child. Gradually, as the Wallaces began to interpret each other's behavior in more constructive ways, they began to reaffirm their ties to each other and to share their grief together as a family. The interpretation of the family's "not caring" about each other was altered as part of the reframing techniques used by the therapist.

Exploring and Expanding the Legacy of the Deceased

Part of resolving a loss involves exploring it. Saying a final farewell to the deceased may not be possible until the bereaved has fully acknowledged that which has been lost. During grief, persons spontaneously evoke memories of their loved one as they attempt to come to terms with their loss. The two techniques presented here, shared reminiscence and ethical wills, enlarge those memories and help the client identify the legacy of the deceased, which they will carry with them throughout their lives.

Shared reminiscence

Reminiscence involves recalling past experiences. In shared reminiscence, people who knew the deceased share their memories and perspectives with each other. It is a normal part of bereavement to talk about the deceased and share the story of the death. During acute grief, individuals will often repeat the details leading up to the death over and over again and listen to others' accounts of it as well, a natural process that helps the person accept the reality of the death. By talking about it, it becomes more real. Reminiscence integrates the cognitive and emotional aspects of grief work and healing (Rosenblatt, 1988).

Shared reminiscing can cover any element of the past. In addition to discussing the death, a variety of other events can be brought up as people share in the memory of the deceased. Using this technique, one can find social support, facilitation of grief work, and an avenue for enhancing relationships with family and friends (Rosenblatt and Elde, 1990). Through this process, individuals sometimes feel that they have gained something (a new perspective on their parent, some treasured stories about one's husband in his youth), which helps compensate for their sense of loss.

Background. Bonanno (1990) talks about the therapeutic aspects of remembering and its reconstructive aspects and observes that "memory is not capable of recording complete events but, rather, stores fragments of information that are reconstructed and interpreted during remembering" (p. 175). Thus, reminiscence is a dynamic process. Shared remembering involves construction and reconstruction of events both individually and jointly until an account is worked out that is "right" and meets the needs of the participants (Gergen and Gergen, 1984).

This technique is especially useful clinically when clients have limited memories of the deceased for a variety of reasons, such as their young age at the time of death. Even adolescents who have lost their parents have many questions about what the parent was like as a person. They may feel that they knew him or her as a parent but not as an individual. Shared reminiscence, either with family members or friends, can help crystallize the identity of the deceased parent. Rosenblatt and Elde (1990) point out that children of all ages may still continue to develop their relationship with the deceased parent even after the death. When the relationship was conflictual, new information can sometimes be gained through shared reminiscence that helps the bereaved make peace with their negative memories.

Suggested guidelines. Photographs and other mementoes are often helpful in activating reminiscence. In some situations, however, it may be difficult to engage in shared reminiscence because of family circumstances (perhaps the client is an only child with little extended family) or unwillingness of family members to cooperate (father may refuse to talk about the mother since her suicide twenty years ago). The therapist can assist the client by suggesting alternative strategies for gathering information. For example, in the case of a middle-aged parent who dies, it might be possible to contact childhood friends, college roommates, or former teachers who can share unique perspectives on the deceased and help fill in the blanks. Many clients find a visit to the hometown of the deceased meaningful. Old documents also have their stories to tell. Scrapbooks and photographs, high school yearbooks, and newspaper clippings can enlarge the mental picture the bereaved carries of the deceased. Exploring the richness of the history of the deceased and the fullness of who was lost by the death helps the bereaved say good-bye to the loved one.

While shared reminiscence is generally a positive experience, clients should be prepared for encountering information that may be disturbing to them. For example, a son may find out that he was adopted and never told, or a widow may find out about an affair that her husband had years ago. The issue of the client's reactions were this to happen should be addressed by the therapist. As the therapist helps the client assimilate the information he or she is acquiring, both negative and positive aspects of this process of review and retrospection will be placed in context and integrated into the person's grief work.

Todd's grandfather, a former physician, died of Alzheimer's disease when Todd was fourteen. As a young child, Todd had been especially close to his grandfather, who lived next door. In many ways the grandfather had functioned as a surrogate parent, since Todd rarely saw his father after he moved to a distant state following his divorce. While he had some precious memories of his grandfather at a younger age, Todd was haunted by the images of the last few years of his life and the dramatic physical and intellectual decline associated with the disease. Therapy with Todd included a review of his grandfather's past and reminiscence about the special relationship they had. Through this process, he was able to hold onto his view of his grandfather as a role model and a person to be emulated, and to diminish the vividness of the images involving the final stages of his illness. In addition, his conversations with his grandmother and family friends provided Todd with specific statements his grandfather had made about him, further validating the strength of their bond.

Ethical wills

An ethical will is a letter or document that shares thoughts and feelings and is left behind for loved ones. Such letters often convey the values and beliefs of the writer and are seen as a crystallization of what the bereaved learned from life. As such, they are treasured by surviving family members and seen as a legacy of love. These letters may also make requests or give advice to survivors (Weizman and Kamm, 1985).

Background. The custom of ethical wills originated in the Jewish culture, although it has been used by other religious groups as well. According to tradition, people should write two wills: one to dispose of worldly possessions and another (of equal importance) passing on their philosophy of life. It was usually written from parents to their children, but other relationships have at times been included. Contemporary ethical wills, as compared to traditional ones, tend to be more informal. They may also be recorded on audio or videotapes instead of being in written form. In addition to a statement of values and words of guidance, there is often an expression of love, appreciation, and validation of children. The Talmud, the document that details Jewish civil and canonical law, states: "Words that come from the heart enter the heart." Even simple messages scribbled on scraps of paper can be precious documents to the bereaved. A variation of an ethical will are letters written at the time of a special occasion or motivated by a crisis in the family (Weizman and Kamm, 1985).

Suggested guidelines. If the bereaved has been left an ethical will (or something akin to one), this document can be used in therapy to reaffirm the ways in which the legacy of the deceased can live on past his or her lifetime. In the event that an ethical will contains instructions or mandates that are at odds with the values of the survivor, the client will need assistance in reconciling these differences. Holding on to love and positive memories while asserting one's right to live one's own life can be a difficult task for grievers.

Most grievers are not left with ethical wills per se, but they can often be found in unexpected forms. If encouraged by the therapist, clients can often uncover old letters, poetry, or other personal expressions of the deceased that make a statement about who that person was and what they valued in life. This may be especially important to a survivor who has not yet reached maturity and may feel a desire from time to time to be comforted by words of advice from someone they loved.

When written documents cannot be located, the therapist can ask the client to imagine having a conversation with the deceased in which their beliefs are discussed. To help facilitate his or her memories, the therapist could suggest talking to relatives who knew the deceased or looking at old photographs. Even when memories are vague, individuals are often able to recall statements, deeds, or incidents that illustrate the keystones of their loved one's character. These recollections can then serve as a guide for constructing an ethical will that the deceased might have written (Weizman and Kamm, 1985).

Weizman and Kamm also suggest writing an ethical will in reverse whereby survivors write a letter to the deceased in which they review how they have been influenced by the loved one who has died, what that person meant to them, and the significance of the individual's life. As important events are recalled and once again shared through memory, the bereaved can give words to thoughts and feelings that perhaps were never voiced.

Maria began seeing a therapist when she became concerned about her inability to make decisions regarding personal relationships. Thirty-two and single, she said she often felt like an orphan, even though she was raised in a large Italian family. (Her father had died four years earlier, her mother five years before him.) While she had always been independent and not especially close to her parents or siblings, she found herself wishing her mother was still alive so she could consult with her about "life." Although acknowledging that she rarely asked her mother's advice when she was younger, she regretted not having listened to her more when she was growing up. She found herself thinking about her mother frequently.

At the urging of the therapist, Maria went through some old boxes from her college days and came across a letter that she barely remembered receiving. It was written by her mother shortly after Maria had broken up with a boyfriend. It read:

The only reason that I hated for you to break up with Carlos is because he loves you so. But, as I told you, you have to think of yourself and your happiness. God knows, you deserve all the happiness in the world. You have always been my little "wise child." I trust your judgment whoever you decide you want to spend your life with.

Remembering this period in her life reminded Maria of a time when she was decisive and more in touch with her feelings. Her mother's words renewed her confidence in her ability to know what was best for herself and to trust her own judgment. The therapist reflected the mother's trusting attitude toward Maria in the following sessions, which helped her feel that she could continue to benefit from her parent's guidance and counsel. Her mother's love and faith in her could still be experienced by recalling the words in that forgotten letter. In fact, Maria said that she felt, in a strange way, a new intimacy with her mother; at the same time, she could rely on her own capacity for making decisions about relationships and move ahead with her life.

Externalizing Grief Through Symbolic Acts

Symbolic techniques can be quite varied, but all involve the therapeutic use of symbols and multiple levels of meaning, and many can have spiritual overtones. Therapists use the creative arts to help clients tap into their inner selves and symbolically represent their feelings, their relationship to the deceased, and/or what that individual stood for. In the preface to her book of poetry, Fritsch (1988) writes about the value of her own creative work following the death of her newborn: "I found that after the creation of a few sculptures, I felt relief as each emotion appeared in clay where I could hold it, caress it and form it into a complete statement of what I was feeling. By adding prose, each became more complete" (p. 4).

Poems, songs, sculptures, and other artistic creations can serve as concrete reminders of more abstract ideas, values, or emotions. These creative works often seem to encapsulate the essence of what the bereaved shared with the deceased. The symbolism contained within can also signify a meaningful psychological passage for the individual or family. In addition to creative works, events or ceremonies containing symbolism are frequently used to represent a transitional step in grief work. The two symbolic therapeutic techniques we have chosen to discuss, rituals and designing symbols of remembrance, can be integrated easily into significant events and are usually readily accepted by those who have suffered loss.

Rituals

Rituals are ceremonial acts that are endowed with symbolic or metaphoric meaning, assisting people through periods of transition and serving as rites of passage. Special people, places, objects, songs, and actions are often associated with important rituals. Kollar (1989) has identified the following four components in the structure of postdeath rituals:

1. *Entry into the time, place, or relationship.* Rituals allow us to enter into a special reality. A ceremony can induce a mood that transcends day-to-day life and offers an affirmation of one's connection to the deceased.

2. *A core symbolic act.* The act can be simple (as in the gesture of reaching out and touching a tombstone) or very elaborate.

3. *Time to absorb what is occurring.* In order to have time to process and fully experience the ritual, segments of time are often allocated to silence, music, or other techniques that reinforce the significance of the symbolic event.

4. *Leave-taking.* The completion of a ritual presents a delicate moment. If it has been meaningful for the participants, and thus successful, the bereaved may find it difficult to end it. It may help to take something tangible from the ceremony. Leaving the scene slowly is also often important in leave-taking.

Background. Throughout the ages, mourning rituals have been used to help people accept the deaths of loved ones. Walsh and McGoldrick (1988) point out that in ancient Mesopotamia, tear vials that resembled miniature bud vases were found buried with the deceased in tombs. The practice acknowledged the emotional significance of the loss and the value of grieving. By burying the tears with the deceased, it also signified the importance of moving on with life.

Because of the symbolic nature of ritual, it can tap into the deeper consciousness of the bereaved and provide an intensity of experience that may be otherwise unavailable. People can process the loss at a core level—oftentimes in an atmosphere of group support—without being overwhelmed by their feelings. It allows the bereaved to translate the loss into an aesthetic expression that is concrete and tangible, while offering symbolism that is comforting to the survivor. The religious nature of many death-related rituals may also help some people connect to a sense of higher purpose and assist in giving meaning to the death. Secular services may be of more value to others who do not have strong religious affiliations.

Postdeath rituals involve more than funerals and memorial services. Sometimes, more private yet more meaningful rituals take place weeks, months, or even years after a death. Activities such as sorting through the belongings of the deceased, removal of a wedding ring, or the scattering of ashes can be very powerful and significant events. For some people, these actions have a transformational power and reinforce the reality of the loss, resulting in positive movement in their grief work. Although the bereaved know intellectually that the person has died, they must come to terms with the loss repeatedly at an emotional level. While postdeath rituals should be encouraged, it is important that they be initiated by the bereaved. Attempts by well-meaning persons to force premature enactment of these rituals can be harmful and actually interfere with the successful resolution of grief.

Suggested guidelines. In order to facilitate a client's progress, therapists frequently help him or her design an appropriate ritual to facilitate the working through of unresolved feelings. Sometimes this is the case after much work has already been done on the issue, and the ritual is used to symbolize the completion of that work and a final "letting go." Other times rituals are incorporated and used throughout therapy to facilitate the mourning process (for example, rituals associated with special holidays or the anniversary of the death).

It is important to assess if the client participated in religious, ethnic, or family rituals at the time of the death. If so, were they meaningful for the individuals involved? Why or why not? Was any individual excluded? If so, for what reason? Kollar (1989) points out that disenfranchised grievers (those whose grief is not recognized or socially sanctioned) may not be included in the ceremonies acknowledging the life and death of the deceased. Gay partners, for example, often find themselves in this situation when parents of the deceased forbid the bereft partner from attending the funeral for fear that others will suspect that their son or daughter was homosexual. Therapists can play an instrumental role in assisting the client to organize a ritual that will substitute for this lost opportunity to openly share his or her grief with others. In this particular circumstance, a special memorial service within the gay community may meet this need.

Rituals designed with the assistance of the therapist should be tailored to and consistent with the unique background, preferences, and needs of the individual. They should be designed to help the individual or family (1) accept the reality of the loss, (2) express feelings related to the loss, and (3) accomplish the tasks of grief work (Rando, 1985). A therapeutically designed ritual might take the form of a visit to a significant place such as the cemetery where the deceased is buried, the location where the bereaved first met the deceased, or the city in which the person died. This kind of pilgrimage seems to be especially important when the bereaved was not physically present at the time of death. The planning and preparation of rituals can be as important as their execution, and with the prompting of the therapist, individuals and families can become highly involved in planning ceremonies that hold special significance for them. The process of designing their own rituals to say their final good-byes to the deceased can facilitate family cohesion and promote support in resolving their shared loss.

> Rebecca's husband had died eleven months earlier and she was only now beginning to feel as if she and her three children (ages nine, twelve, and fourteen) were coming to terms with his sudden death. She expressed to her therapist that she was very proud of herself for having survived the emotional pain of the past year. In anticipation of the approaching anniversary of his death, her therapist asked her what she had planned for that day. Rebecca seemed perplexed and said that she wanted to do something special but nothing that she had thought of had seemed quite "right." When further questioned, Rebecca said that she wanted to do something that acknowledged that she and her children had reached a transition point in their grief: while she knew her grief work was not over, she felt that they had survived the worst of it. The therapist encouraged her to think of past experiences that had been meaningful to her and suggested that she plan an activity (ritual) for that day that incorporated some of the same elements.
>
> Over the next several sessions, Rebecca came to therapy with her children and they discussed what would be important to each of them on this day. Because they had spent many happy times together as

a family at a nearby beach, they all agreed that they would like to return to their favorite spot to reminisce about the past and discuss their feelings of loss. One of the daughters also said that she would like each person to share what the last year had been like for them.

Toward the end of one session, Rebecca recalled her mother telling her about the funerals of her grandparents many years earlier, which involved traditional Jewish customs. (Her mother's side of the family was Jewish, her father's side was Protestant, and she was raised with no religious affiliation. During their marriage, Rebecca and her deceased husband, George, frowned on formal participation in any organized religion. After George's death, Rebecca often thought about her Jewish heritage and on one occasion almost called a rabbi to discuss her deep sorrow over George's death.) In the Jewish tradition, a year after the death is considered a significant marker and is referred to as *yahrzeit*. On this anniversary of the death, an unveiling ceremony is held at the gravesite with family and friends in attendance. The headstone is revealed and loved ones sometimes place stones of varying sizes on the headstone to symbolize the letting go of some of the pain and suffering associated with the loss. Some identification with family traditions seemed important to Rebecca at this point, and she decided, along with her children, to adopt parts of this tradition and use their own version of it at the conclusion of their day at the beach. It was decided that their anniversary day would include collecting beautiful and assorted shells of various sizes and shapes. On the way home from the beach, they would stop at the cemetery and each family member (if they wished) would leave a shell on the grave. As a family, they would reaffirm their love for George and the positive effect he had on their lives. They would also talk about the coming year and the need to leave some of their grief behind as they look toward the future.

Designing symbols of remembrance

Sentiments can be expressed metaphorically through the design and creation of objects or symbols that commemorate the deceased. Having something concrete that represents the memory of the deceased and his or her significance to others can be comforting to those left behind. It can also serve as a focal point for grief work.

Background. The word *symbol* comes from the Greek *sym*, meaning with or together, and *bollein*, meaning to throw or to draw. Symbols do what their definition implies: they draw together and unite experience. Or as May (1975) has said, symbols bridge "the inescapable antinomies of life—conscious and unconscious, reason and emotion, individual and society, history and the present" (p. 703).

The pervasive use of symbols is one of the most distinctive attributes of humans. Symbols act as agents of meaning in all cultures of the world. While the specific meaning attached to any particular symbol may vary among people or cultures, all symbols have one thing in common—they stand for something else. Paradoxically, symbols both reveal and conceal a deeper level of reality and experience simultaneously. They are evocative and suggestive. Symbols have long been recognized as having powerful effects on people, who can be inspired and inspire others through their use (Lewis, 1977). For example, the eternal flame at John F. Kennedy's grave and the Taj Mahal built by Shah Jahan as a memorial to his beloved wife continue to inspire many who see them.

Suggested guidelines. When working with a client to design symbols of remembrance, it is important to recognize that some symbols have universal significance (the sign of a cross), while others have more individualized meaning. Symbols are also culturally relative: a swastika for most Europeans is associated with Nazi Germany, whereas the same symbol reversed means "harmony" among many Native American groups.

Although symbols have cognitive meaning, their force lies in their ability to stir emotion. As Lewis (1977) points out, they are derived both from our hearts and our minds. People often attach significance to objects that are connected to past events but still contain special meaning for them in the present.

What is not generally recognized is that most families, either at the gravesite or elsewhere, create symbols of remembrance that attempt to embrace the essence of the life of the deceased. These symbols are often simple and have meaning only for those close to the deceased. Families having difficulty accepting their loss may not have been able to shift their active grieving into more symbolic form. When used in the context of therapy, symbols of remembrance can help those who are chronically grieving to put some of their grief "outside of themselves."

Families sometimes wait several months, and in some cases years, after a death to place a headstone at the grave, a special symbol of remembrance. The choice of the headstone is extremely important to many people: the design and shape of the monument, the type of material used, and the inscription can all take on special meaning. Other objects placed on the grave or plot (an urn or a shade tree) can have significance as well. When facilitating clients' planning of such symbols of remembrance, be aware that some cemeteries have restrictions on what can or cannot be included.

Ben's wife died of stomach cancer after forty-five years of marriage. During the last months of her illness, he had cared for her at home with the help of Hospice services. In discussing her impending death, Elinor would say, "Now, Ben, I don't want you to go to a lot of fuss after I die. Just a simple service will do." Elinor had a strong religious faith and assured Ben that she was not afraid to die.

Following her death, Ben chose a simple headstone of white marble with the following epitaph selected from the Bible: "The Lord is my shepherd; I shall not want." While Ben said that it gave him great comfort knowing that Elinor was with God and no longer in pain, he said something still felt unfinished. While he accepted the death, he felt a void in his life after so many years of marriage. He missed having someone to look after, and felt that he was no longer needed. In the year following Elinor's death, he started doing volunteer work at his Methodist church. One day he came into a group therapy session with a decidedly more peaceful look on his face. He had planted a rosebush near Elinor's grave over the weekend—a hearty hybrid variety with brilliant red blossoms. His son had gone with him to the "planting ceremony," which provided an opportunity for reminiscence about their shared loss and how much Elinor had loved the beauty of nature. The following year, Ben went to Elinor's grave once or twice a month, pruning and watering the rosebush as necessary. As it bloomed, he would also take some of the flowers to sick friends. Ben never remarried but he was able to reinvest in life and once again experience the joy of living. Nearly eight years after his participation in the grief group, Ben encountered his therapist in the grocery store. One of his first comments was "The rosebush is still alive!"

Selecting Appropriate Techniques

Grief therapy techniques should be selected with a specific purpose in mind. The benefit for the client can include emotional expression, self-understanding and acceptance, externalization of grief, psychological integration of the loss, and instilling hope—all important aspects of effective grief work. As therapy proceeds and the individual begins to reinvest in life, additional interventions may be incorporated that do not focus on grief per se but rather emphasize aspects of readjustment. For example, career counseling may be an important aspect of therapy for the bereaved who are having to reenter the work force after many years of not working. We do not advocate a single approach with all clients, but rather an approach that recognizes common components of grief while still acknowledging the diversity of issues that arise from a loss experience. Recovery from bereavement is a complex process and may therefore require the use of a variety of interventions. The use of specific techniques should depend on the client's needs and the therapist's skill in using them.

CHAPTER 5

Healing Through Group Interaction

I N North American culture, traditional avenues of support for the bereaved have declined over the years. Communities and families, which historically provided care and assistance, are often less available to help with the grief process. For many, the ease of mobility and consequent transient lifestyle have diminished the sense and reality of community. As extended families no longer live together, their members' intimate exposure to the changing seasons of life and the concomitant emotional reactions have become less frequent than in the past. The resulting tragedy is that, too often, individuals have no forum in which to share their grief with others on an ongoing basis, despite the critical role such sharing plays in grief resolution. For some clients a grief group can, to a significant degree, provide this lost opportunity to mourn.

Group counseling and/or therapy can serve as an important adjunct to both individual and family therapy. It can also be used alone as the treatment of choice for some individuals. This chapter explores the characteristics of the group format and the implementation of this approach.

Characteristics of Groups

Because we live in an individualistic society, the benefits of group experiences are often overlooked. In fact, not only clients but many therapists do not understand the power of the group process, which is a forum for change as well as an avenue for meeting basic social needs such as attachment, social integration and friendship, reassurance of worth, reliable alliances, and guidance (Weiss, 1974).

Most disconcerting to the authors is that many mental health professionals with advanced degrees have attended graduate programs where group training was not considered to be a critical skill and thus was not required in the curriculum or even offered as an elective. All therapists function within some type of group or system whether it be family, work, or social. Although the same factors inherent in a therapy group are not always present, group dynamics always exist. Thus, knowledge of and expertise with groups should be part of a therapist's skill repertoire.

To increase the reader's awareness of the unique aspects of group therapy, we begin by examining the basic curative factors within the group setting as discussed by Yalom (1975); all apply to therapy groups and many to the self-help group setting as well. (The differences between these two types of groups are discussed later in this chapter.)

Instilling hope. The client's beliefs that change and health are possible are the basic ingredients of the healing process. These beliefs can be fostered by the confidence expressed by the therapist as well as by observing other group members who are progressing and are closer to the resolution of their grief. These factors help create a faith in oneself, in the treatment, and in a future free from intense pain.

Universality. When we experience intense feelings, we also tend to sense our uniqueness, and this can translate into feeling abnormal and alone. The group experience allows the client to see that she or he is not "crazy" or inadequate. A context of normalcy, even for out-of-control feelings, is created. Yes, every client is unique, but the commonality of the realm of feelings is evident in the group setting.

Information.   The educational component of a group provides a framework into which the griever can fit his or her reactions in order to assess their meaning. The sense that these reactions are appropriate, despite feeling confused and being in pain, can foster a sense of patience with the process and hope for the future. Basic information fills a void since many clients have little insight or information regarding what to expect from themselves during a grieving period.

Altruism and self-efficacy.   The desire to feel needed and important is basic to mental health, and the group experience gives each member the opportunity to feel both. By giving to others, members can regain a sense of personal power and usefulness. In addition, focusing their attention outside of themselves provides a momentary break from personal pain.

Recapitulating the primary family group.   Whenever we interact within a group, or a system, we are likely to respond as we have been taught within our primary system, the family. If this was characterized by unhealthy relationships, then it is likely that the coping styles that developed are also unhealthy. These tend to be inflexible, reflect a poor sense of self, and, inevitably, may not be sufficient to deal with the intense emotional pressure of the grief process. Group interaction can give members the chance to understand their family of origin, explore their consequent adaptive style, and learn how this helps or hinders the grief process.

Developing socializing techniques.   The group setting is ideal for allowing members to offer feedback to each other about their styles of interaction. Even within the context of grief, such feedback can, if used properly, be a catalyst for learning more effective ways to communicate and meet one's emotional needs and for enhancing the ability to develop outside relationships, which furthers the grief process and nurtures self-esteem.

Imitative behavior.   Clients can heal and grow by watching the behavior of other group members and the therapist. Modeling has long been accepted as a powerful learning tool, if the model is respected (Bandura, 1969). We have lost societal models for grieving, and a grief group offers a path for its members to follow.

Interpersonal learning. While the "nature versus nurture" debate contin-ues, there can be no doubt that, to a significant degree, our interpersonal relationships teach us about who we are and how to operate in the world. In a group, each member naturally acts out his or her version of this and is afforded the chance to examine and redefine it in ways that increase the capacity to get the most out of relationships and to feel good about oneself.

Group cohesiveness. As Yalom (1975) points out, it is the affective sharing of one's inner world and the acceptance by others that bonds people in a group. This sense of acceptance allows us to be ourselves fully and, in this case, to experience fully the grief we feel, which eventually leads to resolving the pain.

Catharsis. Expression of intense affect provides a physical and emo-tional release important to the grief process, but it does not stand alone as a stimulus to change. It is a curative component when intertwined with other factors described in this section.

Examining existential questions. Having someone with whom we have had a close emotional attachment die forces us to examine our sense of the meaning of life. Yalom (1975) has suggested that this includes the recognition that life is at times unfair and unjust; ultimately, there is no escape from some of life's pain; no matter how close we get to people, life is still faced alone; only we can take responsibility for how we live our life; and the reality of mortality suggests that how we live life is important.

To move through the grieving process, one must begin to put these awarenesses into some acceptable framework. Without some clarity, death and, consequently, life have no meaning. As Granot (1988) has pointed out, "Working through one's losses means working through one's life, its meaning and how one wishes to live it, with and in spite of the loss" (p. 125).

A group can provide a forum for working on this reassessment of life's meaning. By helping other group members, each individual can regain a sense of usefulness and accomplishment. Members can also become more aware of the limits of what others can give to them. Even within a caring group, they are confronted with the reality of existential aloneness (that is, the ultimate responsibility for making our own choices in life). Given the universality of this experience, the group members can share their work toward acceptance.

Self-help, Counseling, and Therapy Groups

We want to draw a distinction between self-help, counseling groups and what we perceive to be a more intense agent of change, the therapy group. Our intention in this book has been to explore the needs of those mourners who, because of personal issues, need more than the support-ive environment offered in a self-help or counseling group to do their grief work. They need guidance, direction, and even challenge to keep them moving through the process. While these three types of groups have many similar characteristics, they are primarily differentiated by the manner in which members interact and the presence and style of group leadership. In table 5.1 we have drawn the distinction between the poles of a treatment continuum (self-help and therapy) with counsel-ing groups (because of their variability) falling somewhere in between.

Self-help groups

The self-help group movement has grown enormously in recent years, as indicated by the number of community newspapers that pub-

TABLE 5.1
Bereavement Groups: Self-help and Therapy

	Self-help	Therapy
Purpose	Mutual support	Support and professional help with complicated grieving
Size	Unlimited	Maximum 8–10
Leadership	Members	Trained professional(s)
Membership	Open	Specific criteria
Regular Attendance	Not required	Required
Active Participation	Not required	Required
Duration	Open ended	Often fixed time limit
Meetings	Often once a month	Usually once a week
Cost	None	Often substantial

lish extensive lists of local meetings. These groups, when focused on grieving, are usually built around a common theme (widowhood, death of a child, aftermath of suicide) and are designed to (1) assist in helping with the sense of isolation felt; (2) provide education about the grief process; (3) validate the reactions of participants, which can often be looked at as aberrant by the outside world; (4) help with the rebuilding of new relationships; and (5) provide reassurance that mourners can eventually get to a place of resolution (Hudson and Luke, 1988). Folken (1990) has described the major benefits as the chance to meet others with similar issues, a nonjudgmental atmosphere, and learning that one's emotional reactions are normal. Using Yalom's (1975) criteria, we can say that support groups concentrate on the elements of hope, universality, information, altruism, cohesiveness, and catharsis.

Self-help groups make use of the "self-help principle," which implies that "every member of the group should gain insight into problems through independent exertion, with the support of others" (Avort and Harberden, 1985, p. 270). Thus, to profit from the experience, it takes the tapping of inner resources by the individual with the group's help. There is no obligation to do so, however, and no assurance of effective group help if the process becomes complicated.

In a self-help group, attendees are not required to participate. The basic premise—and a correct one—is that they can benefit from hearing and watching others as well as from telling their story or offering help. Over time, as they become more trusting, participants who were reluctant at first often do begin to offer input and gradually profit from this experience.

Counseling groups

As we discussed in chapter 1, a counseling group (as opposed to therapy) provides assistance for the bereaved moving through the process as expected (that is, uncomplicated bereavement). There is a designated leader or leaders and more structure than the self-help format. Although leaders have received training, the depth of this experience varies widely from trained volunteers to professionals with advanced degrees. Counseling groups will include some of the components found in both self-help and therapy groups, depending on the leader's ability or an agency's resources and treatment philosophy.

Therapy groups

A grief therapy group provides a forum for those who are having more than the usual difficulty moving to a resolution of their grief, most often as a result of personal issues other than the grief itself (see the section on complicated grief in chapter 2). While all of the previously mentioned curative factors are found in therapy groups, three of the elements are unique to this format and add to its impact as a forum for change: a focus on recapitulating the primary family in terms of similar behavior within the group, special consideration given to interpersonal learning and socialization techniques, and the challenge of working through existential issues.

Group leadership.   Unlike a self-help group, a therapy group has a designated leader who is usually a mental health professional. The influence and skill of this leader allows him or her to stimulate a powerful interaction process which fosters growth. Yalom and Vinogradov (1988) found that their role as grief group leaders was:

> to anticipate and facilitate a natural process of self-exploration and change, either by staying out of the way of the free-flowing currents of the bereavement groups, or by serving as gentle midwives to themes and concerns that emerge spontaneously during the course of the group work. . . . Rather than dwelling on loss, pain, or emotional catharsis, we found ourselves . . . concentrating on growth, self-knowledge, and existential responsibility. (p. 445)

As the authors point out, "no group can be successfully led simply by stringing together a series of structured exercises" (p. 430). While exercises are a useful element within the therapy setting, leadership requires additional skills, including (1) being well versed in group dynamics and using the group interactional process as a tool for growth, (2) the ability to monitor how each participant is doing and assessing what he or she needs to progress, (3) dealing with clients' resistance to change, (4) using crisis intervention techniques when needed, (5) knowing when to take the lead and when to allow group members to do this, (6) challenging clients not to let their anxiety or fear keep them from dealing with important issues, and (7) knowledge of how one's own issues affect leadership style and decisions.

Choosing the right group

Most people who are grieving can benefit from a self-help or counseling group alone or in conjunction with individual therapy or family therapy. The social support and normalization of the process that is provided in these groups is invaluable. If a client seems to be progressing through the process normally or has exhibited successful coping in the past, one of these modes of help may be sufficient to stimulate and maintain positive momentum toward healing.

Individuals dealing with a complicated grief process, or those looking for more direction than self-help and counseling groups can offer, should participate in a therapy group. If the risk factors for complicated grieving are present, resulting in chronic, delayed, or repressed grief reactions, then a therapeutic approach should be recommended. The therapist should also examine this option for clients at risk of developing "chronic anxiety, depression, psychosomatic illness or drug/alcohol abuse" (Nielson and Leick, 1988, p. 83). For many, current loss brings to the surface unresolved grief from the past, thus adding an element to the healing process that complicates and prolongs grief work.

Criteria for Inclusion in Therapy Groups

At first glance, it might seem strange to raise the possibility that some clients should be excluded from a grief therapy group. After all, if a grief group is designed to help clients through the tasks of the grieving process, then this approach should be used no matter where a client is in that process. The goal of a therapy group, however, is to help clients actually work through grief issues to resolution. To make the most of this experience, as with any type of therapy group, they need to be adequately prepared and possess some basic attributes. Without these, some clients are likely to find the group approach so overwhelming or threatening that they will not stay for long. If a client is not ready for this form of therapy, a self-help group or individual work can be used as a means of helping him or her acquire these prerequisites.

Although the following criteria are important, they are provided only as guidelines and should be coupled with the therapist's own experience and his or her general evaluation of the strengths and limitations of the client.

Acceptance of the loss.   As Worden (1982) has suggested, accepting the fact of loss is the necessary first step in grief work. Clients who are still in a stage of denial or shock are probably not ready for the emotional intensity of their grief and are likely to be overwhelmed or frightened by that of other group members.

Denial can exist on both the emotional level and the cognitive level. Just because clients can verbally and intellectually acknowledge the loss does not mean that they have begun to accept it fully at an emotional level. Yet many clients who are in the midst of this transition can benefit from a group because the experience of others can act as a catalyst for them.

Openness to social interaction.   During the early stages of the grief response, clients sometimes say they just want to be left alone with their grief, without friends and family always around. After a while, the constant presence of "well-wishers" can feel inhibiting. At this point, a client may not be ready to benefit from a group, but once this part of the adjustment period is over, a group could be appropriate.

Motivation to join a group.   Motivation may seem like an obvious inclusion critieria, but it alone is not sufficient; motives for participation need to be explored. The client's expectations of the group experience should be articulated. If they are unrealistic, then the client is unlikely to stay in the group or may turn out to be a very disruptive influence.

One type of unrealistic expectation is the prospective client who wants to be in the group primarily to help others, believing that he or she has found *the* way to handle grief and is eager to teach others. While input regarding personal experiences can be helpful, clients must find their own answers and will resent being told what to think. The resistance encountered is also very disconcerting for the client who is only trying to be helpful. The goal here is not automatically to exclude such clients but to educate them about the parameters of group participation.

Willingness to share.   If a client has always been shy or uncommunicative, a group therapy experience is not likely to be of much benefit. Over time, consistently silent group members can have a censoring influence on the group itself, as other members become resentful that they are sharing and being vulnerable while the quiet one is not. In some cases, however, pressure to participate can become a motivating and healing force, so that an initial assessment of how the client is likely to respond to the challenge is important. Prior coping style is a major clue as to how he or she might react.

Ability to empathize.   Most individuals during the early stages of their grief process are so self-absorbed that they have no energy to give to the understanding of others. For this reason, some Hospice groups require that six months pass after the death before an individual is allowed to join.

Despite the usual pattern of withdrawal after a loss, evidence of prior ability to empathize with others can be an indication that a client is likely to regain this skill in a reasonable time. It is natural for group members to seek help from each other, which can stimulate a revival of this aspect of the bereaved's personality.

Developing a Group

We do not have the space here to present a comprehensive examination of group development; this has been discussed with clarity and in great detail by others (Ohlsen, 1977; Yalom, 1975; Corey and Corey, 1987). Instead, we want to highlight three tasks critical to a therapy group's effectiveness: planning, screening, and preparation of clients.

Self-help groups usually include everyone who is motivated to join. Therapy groups, on the other hand, have as their goal working with people whose grief work is complex and who need an environment that will provide a powerful catalyst for change. To accomplish this, the group leader(s) must carefully attend to all three tasks.

Planning considerations

Before announcing and forming a group, leaders need to ask themselves the following questions:

1. What is the purpose of this group?
2. What types of clients will I include?
3. Will the group be homogeneous or heterogeneous?
4. How long after the death will a client be accepted?
5. What size will the group be?
6. Where will the group be held?
7. What about frequency and length of sessions?
8. How long will the group last?
9. Will members be added or will enrollment be fixed?
10. What is the next step after acceptance for those who will be included?
11. How will clients who are screened but not accepted be handled?
12. How do I feel about a leader's self-disclosure?
13. If a co-leader will be used, how compatible are our styles and values?

Time limits. The decision to offer an open-ended rather than a time-limited group may be dictated more by the needs of the leader(s) or agency than the participants. The open group seems to meet client needs best because of the ongoing support, the ability of older members to assist newer members, and for those who stay on, the chance to more fully resolve universal issues as new members bring them up.

We suggest a blending of these approaches in which the group meets for a specific time—six to eight weeks—and then reassesses members' needs. Those who want to continue can do so, and those who feel they are ready to leave can begin termination with the group. Depending on the preferences of the leader and needs of the clients, those leaving can transition to a self-help group or return on an as-needed basis if the current group will be continuing. Further, the leader can set up a separate drop-in follow-up group to meet periodically. Another option is for the group to end but to plan a future reunion to ensure some continuity.

As the end of a time-limited group approaches, it is critical that the process of termination be addressed in depth, since this new loss will probably bring up new feelings and rekindle previous feelings of grief. Exploration should include a discussion of how it feels to leave, as well as the experience of those who plan to remain.

It is best to allow those group members who stay on to meet again at least once without new members so that they can continue to process termination and transition issues and can be prepared for what will be, in effect, a new group. Remember that the old group had its own "environment" based on members' personalities. It is natural for experienced members to try to establish the same style in the new group, but it will be different to a degree, and this needs to be explored.

Screening interview

The purpose of the screening interview is to assess both how appropriate a client is for the group and of what benefit the group can be to a particular client. In addition to the client's answers to questions, the therapist's observations of the interaction process during the interview can also help assess readiness. Although there may already be assessment data available from another professional, some of the same ground should be covered in the screening as it pertains to group readiness. This process also provides the opportunity to build rapport.

In addition, this is the chance to educate the client about group process, to understand his or her expectations and fears in regard to group participation, and for the client to ask questions of the therapist. It is more than data gathering; it is, in fact, the client's introduction to the therapeutic realm.

Many of the areas to assess have been covered in chapter 2, but there are particular areas that, to a significant degree, relate to a client's ability to use the grief group format. These are listed below.

1. Counseling history, including group therapy
2. Expectations of the group experience
3. Past and current coping skills, including use of medication and drugs, assertiveness, openness to accepting help, self-esteem
4. Assessment of the client's normal group behavior, including whether or not support systems exist and how they are used.

Once an assessment is concluded, we recommend maintaining contact with participants prior to the first group session. The time lapse between screening and beginning can raise a client's anxiety so that she or he might shy away from the first meeting despite the initial interest. Periodic phone calls maintain the connection established during the screening and give the therapist the chance to defuse developing resistance.

Preparing clients for group

Many clients have definite ideas about the appeal of a therapy group, even though they have probably never participated in one. Often the response is "I couldn't handle that now, maybe later." Which usually means, "No way!" Part of this response stems from the North American cultural norms of independence, the tendency to share intense emotions only with family and friends, or the denial of feelings. Sharing with strangers such an intense feeling as being out of control is the last thing a mourner may want to do. How a helper presents this alternative to a client will influence how the client responds.

Since most mourners will not have had prior group therapy experience, helping them to understand what to expect and what is expected of them can facilitate their integration into the group and also increase the power of the group experience. A written presentation of this information can be helpful since, given their emotional condition, they might not remember much of what they are told in the assessment interview. The following guidelines for group participation, derived from the American Association of Suicidology (1990) as well as our own clinical experience, can be given to the prospective members and discussed during the screening interview. It is also wise to go over these again during the norming phase of the first group session.

1. The information shared by group members is confidential.
2. Give yourself a chance. If the first meeting does not meet your expectations, commit to three more before you decide to leave.
3. Intensity of emotion is not the only measure of the depth of a person's grief, so be careful not to compare yourself to others in the group. Everyone's grief is important and unique to him or her.

4. Everyone deserves time in the group and needs to take the responsibility of asking for it if they feel left out.
5. Also keep in mind that the group time needs to be shared.
6. Be open to help from group members, not just the leader.
7. In addition to accepting advice from others, accept your responsibility for finding solutions.
8. Adults learn best by hearing about the experiences of others, not simply by getting advice; therefore, it is usually best to say what *you* did in a similar situation, rather than what someone else *should* do.
9. Share even if you were unhappy about the outcome of some action. It might help someone else avoid repeating your mistakes.
10. Respect the opinions and experiences of others. What doesn't work for you may work for someone else.
11. Inquire to know more about something. Don't try to point out the faults in someone else's thinking or actions.

Components of Grief Therapy Groups

A review of therapist-led groups (Berson, 1988; Knott, 1976; Nielsen and Leick, 1988; Walls and Meyers, 1985; Yalom and Vinogradov, 1988) allows us to draw conclusions with regard to their common features that therapists can use as guidelines for the group experience regardless of the population served.

Discussing norms

Every group begins the first session with a review of the norms as listed above. Group members may want to add to this list or ask for clarification at this time. In addition to the norms, the following logistical issues also need to be addressed:

- The need to inform the leader if a session will be missed
- What to do about smoking and bathroom breaks
- The length of sessions

- The need to be prompt and begin and end sessions on time
- Guidelines about socializing outside of the group

These last two issues require some further elaboration:

Begin and end on time. Ending sessions on time can be difficult, since members may need and want more time and because the expression of such intense emotion is difficult to conclude on cue. There are, however, many reasons for maintaining the agreed-upon session length: (1) grief issues are unlimited and will not be resolved in any one session; (2) the group setting is just one of many places to grieve; (3) members have other commitments besides group, and their time limits need to be respected; (4) constantly going overtime puts the leader at risk of burnout; and (5) to use group time most effectively, members must have a sense of the phases of each session (beginning, middle, end) so that they can participate accordingly. The leader's challenge is to begin to gradually defuse emotions as the session winds down, especially with members who tend to bring up important issues only at the end. If going overtime becomes a weekly problem, it should be acknowledged during a group meeting and ways of dealing with it discussed with the participants.

Socializing outside of group. Unlike support groups, socializing outside of most therapy group meetings is usually discouraged by leaders for a variety of reasons. Among the reasons given is that outside contact detracts from the group sessions as the primary arena of interaction, thus diluting their power and potential impact. We suggest that grief therapy groups break from the norm and that members be advised of the benefits of outside contact to help counteract the sense of isolation that the bereaved feel and actually experience. Feeling connected to others and the world again is an important goal of grief work and one indication of its resolution. Moreover, grieving continues all the time, not just during group sessions. The more support the bereaved receive, the more connected to others they feel and the more likely they are to "reenter" the world and move forward with life. Remember, of course, that while some members will welcome this advice, others will not, so the leader must reiterate that this activity is voluntary.

Introductions

In the first group session, members are usually asked to begin by introducing themselves. This gives each the opportunity to "break the ice," to feel what it is like to be the center of attention, and to get some positive reinforcement for their effort. It also facilitates the connectedness between members as they see the commonality of the expression of grief. A word of caution: the leader needs to monitor the time that is spent doing this because some clients will say just a few words, while others will go into great detail, requiring the leader to decide when and how to redirect and focus on the next client.

In order to achieve the above objectives, the initial introduction can be limited to name, circumstances of the loss, expectations for the group, fears of participation, and anything else that the client feels is important for others to know about him or her. Because this first session can engender great anxiety, it is sometimes easier to do this exercise in small subgroups first and then again in the larger forum. This approach provides time for participants to become comfortable and more able to communicate effectively, since an introduction to just one or two other people tends to be less threatening.

Describing personal loss and bereavement

In addition to the initial introductions, all group members, in one form or another, need the chance to discuss in detail their experiences of bereavement thus far. Introductions allow a brief version of this, but as the group goes on, clients will be open to discussing this in greater detail and need to be encouraged to do so, so that the full realm of their reactions can be explored.

Sharing pictures and anecdotes

Group members tend to feel alone in their sense of loss partly because no one else in the room knew the deceased. Bringing in a picture of him or her and encouraging each to tell the group about that person helps group members feel a deeper sense of each other's loss and gives each mourner the chance to reaffirm his or her relationship with the deceased.

Often humorous anecdotes are recounted and valued personality traits are described. Group members can be encouraged to ask any questions they may have about each deceased person as the picture or memento is passed around.

Learning about the grief process

Normalizing the grief process stimulates participants to fully share with the group because they no longer feel as if their grieving is abnormal. To accomplish this, an educational component regarding what to expect from the grief process is important and usually offered. Pertinent topics include all normal aspects of grief, as well as exploration of possible complications such as chronic physical complaints, suicidal ideation, drug use, or the disappointing reactions of others. Because much of what the group members hear may be forgotten because of their emotional state and initial anxiety over group participation, distributing handouts or books at this point can be helpful. Repetition also serves to deepen understanding and reinforce the important concepts. Eliciting clients' reactions regarding each topic is one means of building group cohesion.

Topic areas

In one way or another these topics should be addressed during the group experience: loneliness, anger, guilt, stigma, changing identity, changing social roles and interpersonal relationships, saying good-bye to the deceased, anniversaries, meaning of life and death, need for rituals, reactions to the group itself, and how family members influence the grieving process. Sometimes the leader can introduce these subjects and ask for discussion, but it is also important to pursue topics that members bring up.

Termination

The ending of a group affords members another opportunity to learn how to deal with grief in a productive way. Encouraging them to deal with any unfinished business toward the deceased, the leader, or each other; to anticipate how it will feel not coming to the group (unless all members return, a new group will be a different experience); to discuss what the group experience has meant to them; to ask for what they want from other members or want to give as they leave; and to discuss their plans for continued support and activity are ways to bring closure to the experience.

Also useful for the group in terminating the sessions is to create some ending ritual either to symbolize what the meetings have meant to them or as a farewell to the deceased. This can be individualized, or the group can design and participate in this together. In a group we recently supervised, each group member was given a flower that represented the deceased. Standing around a table, all members were asked to contemplate the beauty of the flower and how it represented the qualities of the deceased. Then, as a statement that their life must go on without the deceased, they put their flowers into a box in the middle of the table and moved to another part of the room to grieve as needed. The leader volunteered to deliver the flowers the next day to someone who could use them, a symbol of death and rebirth.

Additional Considerations

Besides the group strategies we have already discussed, there are other issues therapists may want to consider, in terms of both specific interventions and style of leadership. In this section we explore situations that, if not dealt with appropriately, can limit the effectiveness of the group process. We also discuss components of group leadership that can enhance the client's experience.

Individual work within a group

The primary power of any group comes from the interaction of its members, but occasionally group members are not responding to a client who needs help or a client is not responding to help from the group. At other times, either one member may continually remain silent or another may take over the group, and no one reacts to this behavior. Leaders have a tendency to fill the void and to deal with the client individually, which is sometimes necessary as a means of modeling and shaping group behavioral norms. But, remembering the purpose of a group (a social interactive forum) and its strength (member interaction), the leader must look for ways to stimulate the group itself to become an active catalyst for change.

In the first example, the leader can reflect back to the group what she or he observes and invite comments. For example, "It seems to me that Cindy is in a great deal of pain right now. I'm wondering if one of us could reach out to her?" To the client who is not responding, the leader can reflect, "Susan, it seems hard for you to take in the caring expressed by group members. What are you feeling now?" or ask the group how they feel about the client's reaction to them. To help the silent client, the leader can observe, "I've noticed that Jim has not said anything this entire session. Has anyone else made the same observation?" When someone responds, ask that person if he or she would like to ask Jim about his silence. If a member is monopolizing group time, the leader can ask the client to pause and then simply ask if anyone would like to comment on what the client has been saying. The basic idea is to deflect interventions back to the group whenever possible.

Leader's self-disclosure

The issue of "leader transparency" (Yalom, 1975) is important to highlight because grief work will invariably stimulate awareness of personal loss issues on the part of the therapist. Working at identifying these issues is imperative. A deliberate decision regarding whether or not, what, when, and how to disclose such feelings to the group must be made both before and during the group's existence. This, of course, speaks to the basic philosophy of group leadership employed.

If accepted as a legitimate therapeutic technique, the leader can determine appropriate timing by always asking himself or herself, "At this moment, is my self-disclosure therapeutic?" That is, "In what way do I expect the group in general or a member in particular to benefit from my disclosure?" If the therapist can answer this question clearly and in the affirmative, then it will probably be helpful to proceed. If the answer is not clear, then we suggest reconsidering such an intervention. With co-leaders present, one can disclose while the other monitors group reactions. When used appropriately, self-disclosure can play a powerful role in helping clients resolve grief, with the therapist becoming a modeling agent. This method is also a means of connecting on a personal level with clients, which can foster the trust that is so crucial to successful therapy. However, therapists who tend to self-disclose without considering the consequences for clients or who often inaccurately assess the impact of such information should seek supervision to explore the dynamics at work.

Clients who fear emotional intensity

Obviously, grief groups are routinely filled with intense emotions, but many clients are not prepared for the degree of intensity they will encounter in themselves or others. Some clients may not be used to it, may have family norms prohibiting such expression, or may simply have a difficult time feeling so vulnerable. For them, the first encounters with such emotionality can be frightening and become the impetus for dropping out of the group very early. Addressing such concerns, therefore, needs to be a regular part of the group preparation and an ongoing process. Some clients have described the weekly grief group as going to the funeral over and over, a description that clearly communicates how difficult it can be to attend regularly. It also may indicate the need to balance out the group experience with some humor and casual socializing.

Addressing secondary issues

Because grieving takes place in the context of a person's personality and past experience, secondary issues—those beyond coping with the current loss—are often an aspect of grief work. The form and complexity that these take can alter the nature of a group significantly. The two examples that follow are illustrative of this point.

Sally had entered a grief group to deal with the death of her sister, who had died as the result of a congenital kidney disease. She felt closer to her sister than to anyone else in the family. During the course of group, Sally began to disclose a history of estrangement from her father whom she hated, a history of attempted suicides (a half dozen times since the age of fourteen), and having been raped. She described a life of emotional isolation and much unresolved hurt.

112

Her self-esteem was very low and despite her disclosures and the efforts of group members to reach out to her, she was emotionally distant from the group and finally dropped out.

Frank's father committed suicide when he was ten years old. His father was an alcoholic and had asphyxiated himself in the garage. By age twenty-nine his grief had still not been resolved because there were so many things to grieve. He felt abandoned by his father, to whom he felt close. Everyone said he looked just like his father and his fear was that he would end up like him. This same image emmeshed his individual identity with that of his father, leaving Frank with a limited sense of self. In addition to great anger toward his mother, he now had periods of intense panic when he felt completely out of control and helpless. At these times he tended to drink heavily in order to calm down.

We have observed that, in most cases, group participants will naturally accommodate to dealing with secondary issues. But though trust between grievers usually is quickly established because of the universality of the experience, this bond can diminish when new material out of a member's realm of experience is introduced. The connection normally found between grievers may not extend to issues such as victimization, suicide attempts, rape, or eating disorders. Conversely, this occurrence can uncover similar personal issues in other participants, which they were not prepared to explore, leading to an emotional or physical withdrawal from the group as a self-protective maneuver.

Depending on the complexity of the secondary issues presented, the type of group process needed to work through them may be somewhat different from grief work, as may the skills and knowledge required of the leader. To assume that the group members will automatically adjust to this increased scope of intervention may be erroneous. The therapist, the client involved, and the other group members must explore together how to proceed.

One approach to this reassessment is for the leader to observe what has happened. For example, "Sally, you have just trusted us with a very important and unexpected aspect of your grieving and I am wondering how you're feeling about dealing with it here in the group?" If Sally is open to moving forward, the leader can suggest that she formally ask the group for assistance. If the group decides to help, then members need to be alerted that their own secondary issues might surface during the subsequent discussions and they should be encouraged to share them if this happens.

If the group is reluctant to help, or if the leader feels that the issues are best dealt with elsewhere, it can be suggested to the individual that she or he begin individual therapy while remaining in the grief group. If leaving the group to pursue treatment is the only viable option, however, time must be spent on termination issues so that all concerned can let go with some degree of acceptance. In this situation, it is the responsibility of the leader to assist the client with the referral.

Training clients to participate

Some clients can inhibit the group process because they are unaware of the impact of their interpersonal style. These are people who espouse religious beliefs they think everyone else should adopt, monopolize the time, cannot accept or work with group feedback and caring, or focus on being a caretaker to others instead of doing their own grieving—all behaviors that will require some intervention by the leader directly or through the use of group reaction.

In groups with a religious affiliation, the application of a narrowly defined approach to grieving is appropriate. General grief groups, however, need to remain flexible to the unique needs of each client. For the client who feels the need to adopt a teaching role, the following is an intervention that is usually helpful. "I think it's wonderful that you've found a sense of meaning that works for you, but remember that we all have to find this for ourselves." A more challenging technique is to ask the receiver, "Sid, I'm wondering how you feel about Mary's advice." Or the leader can ask the group the same question. The goal is to help the advice-giver get a sense of how he or she is being perceived.

Some people are so emotionally distraught that once they start expressing themselves they have difficulty stopping. Sometimes this is the person's personal style and is unrelated to the grief work. It is a judgment call on the part of the leader as to when this is becoming disruptive to the group, and difficult as it may be to redirect the group away from a client in obvious need, the needs of the group must also be considered. The therapist can ask the client, "Peter, I know you have much more to say, but I wonder if it would be all right with you if we come back to you at another time so that others can get their chance today?" or "Peter, we need to move on today. Is there something that we can do briefly that would help you at this moment?"

Clients who seem to sidestep group feedback regarding their behavior or discount members' expression of caring are usually dealing with issues of self-esteem or other unresolved pain. A leader might start by pointing out this tendency and asking the client how he or she feels when others offer feedback or express their concern. The sender can also be asked how he or she feels about the receiver's response.

Dealing with multiple loss issues

When a client is not moving through the grieving process, it could be that the current grief has touched off older unresolved grief issues.

Judy's fiancé died five years ago in a freak sky-diving accident (his parachute failed to open and he fell thousands of feet to his death). Judy has had no close relationships since then and cannot let go. She describes Tom as her best friend and soul mate—they did everything together. Her tears flow and the pain she expresses to the group makes it seem as if the death had occurred yesterday.

Why is Judy's grief so current? Why has she been reluctant to connect with anyone else romantically? Judy's parents divorced when she was seven years old. She says it didn't bother her at all. She just "toughed it out" and learned to become self-sufficient; thus, in effect, she never grieved over the divorce. Tom's death triggered long-buried feelings of abandonment. If we look at her description of her relationship, we can hypothesize that her closeness with Tom took the place of her lost ideal parent. Losing him brought up unresolved feelings of losing a parent, which have still not been addressed.

Understanding what factors are at work when clients are stuck requires a careful assessment of their history with loss and the willingness and skill of the leader in opening the doors to unfinished business.

Using touch

In Western society we tend to touch or hug in an effort to communicate our caring for someone who is hurting. Or if there are tears, we offer a tissue. Therapists need to keep in mind that the meaning of such gestures is not universal. Some clients will interpret them as warmth and support; others will find them threatening or a message to stop their emoting. For example, as children, our mothers hugged us to make the hurt go away. Offering a tissue might have communicated, "Dry those tears and stop crying; everything will be all right." But we can't take away another's grief, and crying is part of the healing process, so leaders should be sensitive to how their actions are perceived and take their cue from the client. Ask if holding the client's hand while he or she cries, for example, is desired before you proceed. Most of the time we have found clients very receptive to such an offer, but in one extreme case a client panicked when another group member put his arm around her to console her. She had been molested as a child and the unexpected touch acted as a flashback mechanism.

Using a process observer

A process observer sits in a group without participating (Yalom, 1975; Zieman, Romano, Blanco, and Linnell, 1981). His or her task is to take notes about what occurs in the group (observations of the interactive process between members and interpretations of what is happening). Group members are given a written summary of these notes to examine the week after the session. The benefits are many: a fresh perspective on what actually happened, a concrete method of monitoring group progress, maintenance of the group connection during the week, highlighting important themes that need to be carried over, helping the leaders to plan strategy, and helping members get a perspective on themselves that they can work with in the next session.

Although the use of a process observer is not always feasible, his or her inclusion in the group can have great impact. This exercise also serves as a training method for future group leaders, since it allows the observer to focus on the group process exclusively, without the complex responsibility of both the leadership and participant roles.

References for Specific Types of Grief Groups

In this chapter we have discussed the aspects of grief therapy groups in general, but how these elements are uniquely applied to specific types of loss is also important. We refer you to the following examples of how these principles have been used in self-help, counseling, and therapy groups: suicide (Hatton and Valente, 1981; Lukas and Seiden, 1987; Wrobleski, 1984); surviving partners of AIDS victims (Klein and Fletcher, 1986; Land and Harangody, 1990); college students (Knott, 1976; Berson, 1988); widows (Nachmias, 1988; Redburn and Juretich, 1989); family intervention (Elde, 1986); general self-help and support groups (Spiegel, 1980; Schwab, 1986); death of a newborn (Wheeler and Limbo, 1990); women in prison for the death of a child (Kaplan, 1988); Hospice bereavement groups (Buell and Bevis, 1989; Rognlie, 1989); delayed grief (Davidsen-Nielsen and Leick, 1988).

CHAPTER 6

Individual and Group Intervention with Children and Adolescents

MOST books on grief therapy focus on adults and ignore the special needs of younger clients. A variety of approaches to working with bereaved children and adolescents have been developed and are currently in use. These approaches include both individual and group interventions.

Psychotherapy with Children and Adolescents

Working with younger clients in a psychotherapeutic setting requires an understanding of developmental principles. Therapy integrated with a developmental perspective permits the full utilization of age-appropriate interventions. These interventions, when used effectively, serve as a catalyst for growth and change.

Mechanisms of change

Freedheim and Russ (1983) have identified a number of variables within the therapy process that effect change in children and adolescents: catharsis and the labeling of feelings, insight and working through, corrective emotional experience, learning alternative problem-solving and coping strategies, and development of an internal structure. In addition, healing may be facilitated when young people feel that they are no longer facing their problems alone.

Catharsis and labeling of feelings.　Helping clients to identify and understand their feelings is a major goal of therapy, and helping them to feel safe expressing themselves is an important task of the therapist. Expression of negative feelings can be especially problematic for bereaved children and adolescents. In the context of therapy, they get their emotions out in the open so they can begin to deal with them. The therapist labels and reflects what he or she detects from the child's voice, body posture, or verbal statements. Connecting words to feeling states make them more manageable for young clients and less overpowering.

Insight and working through.　In order to develop insight, behavior is linked to feelings and thoughts by way of interpretations made by the therapist. For example: "When you feel sad and sense that your sister and mother are sad too, you sometimes start an argument so that the sadness will change to madness, because you think it hurts less." Once interpreted correctly, the behavior becomes more understandable and the young client also feels understood by the therapist. Cognitive abilities must be taken into consideration when offering explanations to children and adolescents. Younger children are less capable of cognitive mediation than are older children, and school-age children are less able to think in abstractions than are adolescents. *Working through* refers to the process whereby ambivalent emotions and conflicts are confronted and resolved. This process in children occurs through repetitive play or other activities which allow them to come to terms with painful events or situations.

Corrective emotional experience.　A corrective emotional experience allows the young person to express a negative emotion and receive a response that does not meet the expectation of punishment or rejection. The relationship between the young client and the therapist is crucial for a corrective emotional experience to occur. For example, if an adolescent reveals that she sometimes hated her deceased sister because she got all the attention, the therapist should be accepting of the feeling and help

the teenager understand the reasons behind the feeling and that ambiva-
lence is a normal part of sibling relationships. Such hidden feelings are
often revealed only after a trusting relationship has been established
with the therapist. After a series of these types of interactions, children
and adolescents have less guilt and anxiety about their feelings and
impulses and are less judgmental about themselves.

Learning alternate problem-solving and coping strategies.   The ability to
effectively cope and problem solve are crucial to the recovery of the
bereaved child and adolescent. Most young people have limited experience coping with crises, especially ones related to death, and consequently they usually have a limited range of coping skills. In the context
of therapy, they can develop skills that will help them cope with the
intensity of their feelings (asking for affection and support from parents)
and handle difficult situations (dealing with teasing on the playground).
The therapist may be directive and suggest a solution to a particular
problem or may present an alternative way of viewing a situation as a
means of coping.

Developing an internal structure.   Some bereaved children and adolescents may have experienced early developmental problems and will
consequently need help in fostering an internal structure that will facilitate positive development in the future. This internal structure includes
a sense of self, an acceptance of self, and the ability to regulate emotional
and behavioral responses in an age-appropriate manner. For clients with
difficulties in these areas, the therapist can help develop the cognitive
and affective functions related to self-esteem regulation, impulse control,
reality testing, and differentiating self from others.

Methods of intervention with children

Play therapy.   Play is a natural medium of self-expression for children.
It can be used for diagnostic understanding, to establish a relationship
with the child, and to elicit material that will reveal the child's anxieties,
fears, and defenses. It also has a cathartic effect because conscious and
unconscious material is acted out through play, thereby relieving accompanying tension. Finally, children use play as a means to express, relive,

reenact, sublimate, and test reality. Mishne (1983) summed it up well when she said, "Play activity is a complex kaleidoscope of the child's conscious and unconscious expressions" (p. 285).

Play may be directive or nondirective. While there are a variety of therapeutic approaches to play therapy, in nondirective ones the therapist usually provides a variety of prompts (toys) and encourages the child to engage in spontaneous play. Directive approaches are more structured, oftentimes with a specific intent in mind. The following example of a role-playing activity illustrates this point: Prior to the session, the therapist had limited success in identifying the child's primary issues. (The child's father had been killed in a motorcycle accident a year earlier.) Because of the young age of the child, a direct questioning technique did not hold the child's attention and yielded little useful information. (Children often do not respond to direct questions about their feelings.) Through a creative role-reversal exercise, the therapist was able to obtain important information about the child's fears and concerns.

> When three-year-old Julie arrived at the session, the therapist told her they were going to play a special game. They would change places, and Julie would pretend she was Dr. Cook, and Dr. Cook would be Julie. Julie asked, "Do I get to sit in your chair and everything?" After receiving an affirmative response from the therapist, Julie climbed up into the swivel chair, assumed a very mature posture, and started organizing the papers on the desk in front of her. The therapist meanwhile took Julie's usual place on the couch and asked, "Well, Alicia, what do you want to ask me today?" Without hesitation, the child started asking questions: "Why do you cry at night when everyone is asleep?" "Don't you know that you will get spanked if you cry?" Then she said, "Your sisters are mean because they remember your Daddy and you don't."
>
> In this role reversal, the therapist said little. When a response was required, the therapist would look to Julie for guidance and ask "What am I supposed to say?" suggesting that she was inexperienced at playing pretend games. Julie would then laugh and fill in with the "right" response. At the end of the session, the therapist praised the child for her efforts and thanked her for teaching her how to play the game. Through the use of this technique, the child gained much

enjoyment from the interaction and the therapist gained a great deal of insight into Julie's internal thought processes and feeling states. A secondary benefit of this session was the contribution it made to Julie's feeling of self-esteem. During the next several sessions, the therapist followed up with play therapy and parent counseling.

Sugar (1988) provides an excellent example of the use of play therapy with a preschooler following an air disaster. He shows how the child's particular situation and developmental stage are critical elements in therapy.

Use of games. Whereas preschoolers seem to especially enjoy role play (or "pretend play"), older children and adolescents usually prefer structured games. The phrase "it's just a game" is a powerful psychological cue for the loosening of restraints and relaxing of defenses. Games, because they are familiar, can help children feel more comfortable and engage them in the therapeutic process. In their book *Game Play: Therapeutic Uses of Childhood Games*, Schaefer and Reid (1986) provide an excellent discussion of therapeutic games, including communication board games; a talking, feeling, and doing game; self-understanding games; and problem-solving games. (Several of them have been adapted for use on computers.) These games are designed to teach children how to express feelings, to help them discuss and cope with their problems and fears, and to enhance their self-esteem.

In general, the more structure and rules a game has, the less therapeutic value it will have. Also, games selected for use in therapy must easily fit into the session length and allow ample time for spontaneous discussion. We often use games as an impetus for discussion in therapy, and by the end of the session both the children and therapists have usually forgotten about finishing it. Other therapists with different styles may use games in a more strategic way.

Storytelling. Storytelling techniques can be used with children of all ages. Most young people are familiar with this mode of learning about others' lives. In fact, much of our everyday conservation is built around telling stories of one sort or another (what a neighbor did last week, what happened at the park). Used in therapy, storytelling can be a nonthreatening way for a child to reflect on feelings, to be exposed to alternative perspectives, and to feel that others have been in his or her situation (Smith, 1989). Stories can hold a child's attention and are easily remembered. As James (1989) points out, "Metaphor embedded in story is a powerful teaching tool and a good way to transmit empowering messages" (p. 212). Following is an example of the metaphorical tales that she shares with traumatized children: "The brave knight who sensibly wore his armor in battle and felt so comfortable and safe that he began to wear it all the time, became so accustomed to it that he eventually forgot he could take it off. He had all sorts of silly misadventures clanking around in his safe, but not always necessary, protection" (p. 212). Metaphors are fun for children and encourage active participation as well as provide a safe way of exploring frightening feelings. Important messages can be conveyed to the child through the use of this technique (James, 1989; Mills and Crowley, 1986).

Although the therapist is often the storyteller, this role can be shared. Gardner (1971) has discussed the efficacy of his mutual storytelling technique for helping children improve communication, gain a sense of mastery, and resolve conflicts. Following a death, children, like adults, have their own stories to tell, and sharing them with others can be therapeutic. They often like to give their stories a degree of permanence and increased importance by writing them down. We frequently help children do this in the form of a booklet and find that most of them are eager to add illustrations as well. If a child is too young to write the story, the therapist can serve as the recorder while the child dictates.

Methods of intervention with adolescents

Writing.   Writing during bereavement has been shown to be therapeutic (Lattanzi and Hale, 1984), decreasing the intensity of feelings through "giving grief words" and helping the person gain a different perspective on a disturbing event (McKinney, 1976). Adolescence is a period in which writing skills are developing as advanced cognitive skills are acquired, and many teenagers keep journals, try writing poetry or songs for the first time, or correspond with a friend or relative. They are experimenting with putting thoughts and feelings in written form, making it a natural avenue to explore one's feelings of loss.

Therapeutic writing can take many forms. Writing a letter to the deceased is a common technique used in grief therapy, allowing the bereaved to focus on hitherto unexpressed feelings. It can be an opportunity to say goodbye to the deceased if the adolescent was not able to do so prior to the death. Letters can also be used to "make peace" with the deceased if the relationship had been a conflictual one. Parent-child relationships during adolescence often include some degree of conflict as a son or daughter struggles to achieve individuation and autonomy, so the death of a parent during this stage can leave an adolescent with feelings of remorse.

Diaries or journals can also be therapeutic means for expressing feelings without fear of reprisal or judgment. The translation of experience into language helps the person assimilate and integrate it, since the process of writing is slower than talking and gives more opportunity to get at the core of feelings. It also provides documentation of a mood or feeling state. When adolescents are encouraged to keep a journal during the course of therapy, they are often impressed with their growth when they go back and read entries made several months earlier. This reinforces their sense of progress and validates the difficult journey they have taken in their recovery from bereavement.

Music.   In order to do effective therapy with adolescents, therapists must tap into their world, and music plays an important role in the lives of most youth. Aubrey (1977) has emphasized the need to accept the adolescent's own way of coping with a loss and observed that many adolescents when sad or depressed almost automatically turn on their radio or stereo. Attig (1986) suggests that music serves as an alternative frame of reference, apart from family, school, or church, through which their concerns can be addressed. It affords opportunities for identification with situations, ideals, hopes, and aspirations. Communicating with teenagers through music can enhance the therapist's understanding of the client's point of view. According to Attig, "Cultivating such understanding is akin to learning and using a foreign language in a foreign country. It serves as a means of exchange of ideas and issues. The very attempt to understand says much about the genuineness of the act of reaching out" (p. 33).

Loss, grief, and bereavement are common themes in adolescent music (Attig, 1986). For every bereaved person, certain songs or compositions elicit feelings, thoughts, and memories related to the lost relationship.

The reactions are immediate—as soon as the music is heard, it serves as a cue to stir associated emotions. It can be an intense experience, eliciting powerful emotions as the music stimulates the client to recount poignant moments involving the deceased.

Advocating the use of music in therapy, Lochner and Stevenson (1988) emphasize that music is a vehicle for accessing deeper levels of thought and feeling: "Music is a *tool*. It can help a person to move into the world of symbols and to share that experience with someone else. It can break through defenses, put both parties in touch with their feelings and give shape and substance to those feelings" (p. 174). We advocate that adolescents be encouraged to select the music they would like to use in therapy. It may be played in the session or simply discussed as particularly meaningful lyrics are recalled.

Adolescents may want to write their own music in tribute to the deceased. One young client who lost her best friend to cancer wrote a song attesting to their special friendship. It met her need to "do something" in response to the death and embodied the essence of their friendship through its expression of trust, sharing, and pleasure. She sang and played the song at the memorial service at the request of her friend's parents, thus further adding to her sense of contribution and connection.

Groups for Bereaved Children and Adolescents

Therapy and support for bereaved children and adolescents in the professional literature has focused on individual treatment, and few guidelines exist for addressing the concrete and practical issues involved in conducting groups with younger clients. Surveys conducted by the American Group Psychotherapy Association have shown that less than 1 percent of all groups conducted by psychotherapists are for children, and only a small number of child therapists in private practice organize children's groups (MacLennan, 1986). Increasingly, however, Hospice and other organizations are recognizing the need for bereavement groups for all age levels, and numerous groups for children and adolescents are currently in operation across the country. The goals for these groups are generally to provide peer group support, to educate about death and grief in an effort to avoid misunderstandings and misconceptions, to facilitate normal grieving, and to prevent pathological grief reactions.

Benefits of group experience

The question is often asked, "Can children benefit from groups?" Our experience leads us to conclude that participation in a group can be a very important component of therapeutic intervention with bereaved children and adolescents for the following reasons.

Peer relationships. Peer relationships, an important part of youth, assume increased importance as children move from the early years of life through the school-age years to adolescence. Children and adolescents are accustomed to functioning as part of a group in their families, at school, in clubs, and in sports, so the normal developmental need for peer involvement can be met through the group process found in therapy and support groups. Young people will often more readily share their feelings and concerns with friends than with adults, and contrary to what many adults think, they can and do offer emotional support to one another.

Support. Children are often forgotten grievers, especially younger ones. After the loss of a family member, they may have less accessible emotional support from significant others than prior to the loss. As Masterman and Reams (1988) point out,

> The death of a parent entails many stressors for the child besides grief. The surviving parent is often deeply involved in his or her mourning and may be unable to provide the emotional and physical care needed by the child. Frequently, financial difficulties following a death may force a formerly nonworking mother to seek employment, or force the sale of the family home with the resulting loss of support from neighbors, school, and friends. Painful emotions surrounding a death can also damage relationships with the extended family. (p. 563)

Being a member of a group can add to children's sense of support and give them a special place to share their feelings.

Normalization.   Following the death of a loved one, many children and adolescents report feeling different from their peers. Knowing and interacting with others who have had similar experiences can reduce these feelings of alienation and perceived isolation. It can also give them the opportunity to share feelings in an environment in which they think others will understand and accept them and to identify with those who are successfully coping with their losses.

Venting of feelings.   The group can be a place where they are encouraged to be youngsters and express their feelings in an age-appropriate way. James (1989) discusses the concept of the "parentified child," which is sometimes manifest after a family experiences a traumatic event. Viewing their grieving parents as vulnerable and in need of protection, children and adolescents sometimes do not look to parents to have their own needs met. In fact, they often sacrifice their own need to grieve in an effort to spare their parents because they think that talking about their own grief will just upset them more. Hogan (1987) has used the term *camouflaged grief* in describing the concealment of feelings about the loss. In extreme situations, the child may even try to function in the parental role and feel responsible for the grieving parent's welfare. The needs of these younger family members go unrecognized because they are so adept at meeting adult needs and hiding their own fears. Many "parentified children" do not have well-developed play skills or social skills, and groups can encourage and foster these skills in a setting involving peers. In individual therapy, therapists tend to relate to younger clients, especially adolescents, on an adult level, thus reinforcing that role. In a group setting involving their peers, children and adolescents are given permission to just be themselves.

The following conversation, which took place in a children's grief group (Vastola, Nierenberg, and Graham, 1986, pp. 83–84), shows how these four goals of a group—peer interaction, support, normalization, and venting of feelings—are effectively met.

TIM: I have some stuff that I brought in—the stuff you wanted to see.

MATT: Well, what is it?

TIM: Well, this is the paper that they passed out from the church. It has my grandfather's picture on the cover . . . and inside it says he was in the army . . . and he had three children and twelve grandchildren . . . and over here it tells you to pray for him. And this is a scrapbook from where he worked as a security guard, and his picture here in the security uniform.

GLORIA: He was a handsome man.

TIM: *(Rather wistfully)* He was.

LEADER: It sounds like he did many things in his life—being in the army, and a security guard . . . [having] three children and twelve grandchildren.

TIM: He did.

CARL: Was he nice?

TIM: Yup. I used to go see him sometimes. And he had a dog. His dog died before he did.

LEADER: Sounds like you miss him.

TIM: *(Fighting back tears)* I do. Now I can't go see him anymore.

GLORIA: Dag.

LEADER: What do you mean by that?

GLORIA: That's a shame.

LEADER: What?

GLORIA: That his grandfather died, and he can't go see him anymore.

LEADER: It sounds like a sad thing.

GLORIA: It is. *(Tim nods.)*

Role of the leader

A leader should have knowledge of group dynamics and small group process as well as experience working with a variety of age levels. In addition, effective leadership requires familiarity with children and adolescents and their means of expression, their understanding of death, and their ways of grieving. We advocate that therapists focus on a particular age group since the skills required to work with preschoolers, for example, can be quite different from those needed to work effectively with adolescents. Regardless of age of group participants, the group leader needs to:

1. Be familiar with developmental characteristics of children and adolescents and plan activities that are congruent with their age levels and abilities
2. Be creative in terms of introducing activities that are age-appropriate, that will maintain interest, and that promote self-expression
3. Model the verbalization of feelings and needs to set a norm for the group, and encourage this behavior among group members
4. Recognize and respond to both verbal and nonverbal communication during the sessions
5. Provide structure while allowing room for spontaneity and participant-generated discussions

Leaders typically take more of an active role in children's groups than in groups for adolescents or adults. Older adolescents like to feel a sense of control in the group regarding its focus and structure. Seeking their input and involving them in decisions can strengthen their investment in the group. Even younger children typically like to personalize "their group" in some way. One way to achieve this is by having the children decide on a special name for the therapy group. In one such group, a young boy suggested the name "The Lost and Found Group" because, as he said, he had lost his mother and was trying to find her (Vastola, Nierenberg, and Graham, 1986).

Common group themes

Bereaved youngsters often have common concerns related to their loss. Following are five common themes that can be expected to emerge in groups of bereaved children and adolescents:

1. *Feelings of sadness and despair.* Deep feelings of longing for the deceased loved one may be expressed as they mourn their loss. Children and adolescents may cry, look visibly depressed, or show other overt signs of sadness.

2. *Worry about other family members dying and concern over who will take care of them.* Along this vein, children may fantasize about further abandonment and separation. These fantasies can add to their already heightened sense of fear and anxiety and cause temporary regression in their behavioral development (reverting to bed-wetting or thumb-suck-

ing). Consequently, these children need reassurance that they will continue to be loved and cared for. Adolescents may feel that they have to "make it on their own" and assume adult responsibilities earlier than anticipated. While previously rebelling against authority, the adolescent may now feel the void left in terms of parental guidance if a parent is the one who has died.

3. *Anger about their loss and the resulting disruption in their lives.* These feelings sometimes erupt at school and result in problematic behaviors such as playground fights, hostile remarks to teachers, fast driving. Intense emotions need to be explored and given expression in a way that is not detrimental to the youngster.

4. *Feelings of guilt over whether they caused or contributed to the death.* Parents often make thoughtless remarks such as "You are worrying me to death," not realizing that children might take these comments quite literally should the parent consequently die. Guilt reactions are often hidden from others because of the deep feelings of horror and shame associated with them. Feelings of guilt may also be associated with the last time they saw their loved one alive, especially if it involved disobedience or misbehavior on the part of the child. Even adolescents, because they do not have the maturity to put the death in perspective, may feel that they contributed inordinately to the death. Since adolescent-parent relationships are at times strained, some teenagers may feel that lines of communication are not open to explore their feelings surrounding this issue with the remaining parent.

5. *Questions about death and dying.* Leaders should be prepared for the straightforward questions of young children, which can sometimes be disturbing to adults, such as "Do worms eat you all up when you're in the grave?" Cook and Oltjenbruns (1982) also found important differences between the questions and concerns asked by junior high students as compared to high school students, reflecting differences in their cognitive-developmental levels. For example, the questions of junior high students tended to focus on concrete events and physical appearance ("How much did the funeral cost?" "What did they do to my brother after he died?" "Do the muscles and stuff still move after a person is dead?"). In contrast, high school students asked more abstract questions seeking a deeper level of understanding ("Why did Grandmother want to be cremated?" "What is the best way to show my teacher that I am sorry about his wife?").

Considerations in planning

Communication with parents.   Contact with parents throughout the therapy process is critical. Initial conferences are generally held with each participant's parent(s) to explain the objectives of the group as well as the format and rules of operation. At the end of the group experience, a termination meeting is usually held in which the child or adolescent's progress is evaluated. For preschool and school-age youngsters, Masterman and Reams (1988) suggest that when parents come to pick up their children after a session, they be told what the general topic of discussion has been that day, how it was presented, and how the children reacted. Parents can then be prepared for related questions and comments during the week.

Cunningham and Matthews (1982) have proposed a parallel group format in which parents and children meet together once a month and separately in parent's groups and youth groups, respectively, the other three weeks of the month. The joint sessions allow therapists to become more familiar with each client's parent(s) and possibly other family members. These sessions also offer therapists the opportunity to work on improving parent-child interactions and to obtain additional information on the youngster's progress at home, at school, and with peers outside the group. The separate sessions allow both parents and children to explore their own issues with less inhibition. Parents are often reluctant to discuss certain personal issues in the presence of their sons and daughters (such as sexual adjustment after loss of a spouse), and children and adolescents may not fully exhibit peer behavior with a parent present (Gaines, 1986).

A less formal option is to facilitate interaction among parents of group participants by having a comfortable waiting room where parents may wait during the group session. This setting provides parents with the opportunity to interact with each other and share common concerns regarding parenting following bereavement. If parents of group members are acquainted, it will also help children who want to maintain contact with other group members following termination of the group (sometimes deep friendships develop out of the experience). Educational materials placed in the waiting room can also serve as a resource to parents.

Space and equipment needs. Children and adolescents require more space than do adults because of their overall activity level and the participatory nature of each session. Young children learn and express themselves through play, and a limited physical space can restrict such expression. MacLennan (1986), however, stresses that boundaries are important in group therapy with children, and that, in general, large gymnasiums or limitless outdoor spaces are unsuitable because they allow for group fragmentation and provide insufficient structural support. On the other hand, he points out, too small a space can violate a child's sense of personal space and create anxiety. Adolescents need a space in which they can spread out, sitting at a distance from others when they prefer. Additionally, children and adolescents need to feel a sense of privacy in the space and a degree of ownership, which can be fostered by having objects in the room with which they can identify. For example, young children might like to see pictures of their favorite cartoon characters on the wall, whereas this would be offensive to adolescents, who would prefer posters of current rock stars or athletes. It is a common practice to modify rooms for use with different age groups. When working with young children, a safe environment is also important, and attention must be paid to breakable objects such as glass in the room.

The appropriateness of furniture will vary according to age level. Furniture should be child-sized for young children, but if this is not possible, they usually feel comfortable sitting on the floor with their group leaders. An appropriate physical environment will also include evocative toys and other prompts that give children opportunities to express themselves through action, words, or symbolic play. Adolescents, on the other hand, prefer an informal setting to feel comfortable. Large overstuffed chairs and couches or pillows are ideal for this age group. Various age-appropriate reading materials scattered about will help give them a sense of belonging.

Setting. As mentioned earlier, few groups for children or adolescents are offered in private practice settings because it is difficult to bring together a large enough number of suitable clients in the same age range at any given time. When private practice therapists do conduct groups, they tend to advertise them broadly in the community and receive referrals from other practitioners. Community agencies and mental health centers are settings in which groups for children and adolescents are more frequently seen. Hospice programs, for example, come in contact with a large number of young people affected by grief. Most hospices offering such grief groups do not restrict participation to those with family members previously receiving their services.

Specialized health-care facilities are also appropriate settings for some programs. Siegel, Mesagno, and Christ (1990) describe a grief support program they offer through the Sloan-Kettering Cancer Center. Their psychoeducational program uses a parent guidance model to prepare children for the death of a parent, facilitate children's adjustment to the loss when it occurs, and assist the surviving parent in his or her transition to single parenthood. Intervention begins about six months before the anticipated death of the parent with cancer (as estimated by the patient's physician) and continues for four to six months following the loss. The eight sessions, spaced two to three weeks apart, involve five sessions with the well parent alone, one or two with each child in the family alone, and one with the well parent and children together. (In some situations, the ill parent is included in a limited number of sessions as well.) Adaptations of this model could include groups for children and adolescents from different families.

Increasingly, school systems are providing therapeutic services for students. Groups are a very efficient way to address personal concerns that are affecting school learning and behavior. The recent trend has been toward the use of issue-specific groups within the schools—for bereaved children, for children of divorce, for adolescents with chronic illness. Many schools have well-trained psychologists and counselors qualified to work with mental health issues. Crisis groups have also been formed when a large number of students in one locality experience loss (for example, a tornado striking a small town and resulting in fatalities, a rash of adolescent suicides occurring in a community, children witnessing a murder on the playground). Haran (1988) gives an interesting account of a single-session group used to provide intervention for classmates of a nine-year-old boy murdered by his father. Other group intervention efforts may involve children or adolescents who are not directly affected by a death. For example, in an effort to help bereaved children by increasing the empathy of their classmates and sensitizing them to loss issues, Balk (1989) used guided fantasy in a classroom context with fourth- and fifth-grade children.

Suggested guidelines

Homogeneity of group. In most circumstances, an age span of three to four years is best, especially when preschool children are involved. Additionally, we rarely include school-age children in a group for adolescents; adjustments for widely varying developmental differences and accompanying needs of group members representing diverse age groups can be counterproductive. The exception to this is forming special groups for siblings, composed of several children from the same family. Despite age differences, they have all shared a common loss, which adds focus to the group.

In general, homogeneous groups (those having only bereaved participants) tend to be more cohesive and offer more immediate support (Mishne, 1983). It may sometimes be better to refer young clients to a general adjustment group in which peers are learning to cope with a variety of issues (divorce, death, separation) rather than to place them in a grief group that has few members their own age. The choice of a homogeneous versus a heterogeneous group must also be determined by the therapeutic goals for the individual child or adolescent.

Size of group. The group size is strongly influenced by the age of the participants. Groups for preschool children should be limited to six or fewer, depending on the characteristics of the particular children involved and the availability of a co-leader. Four or five members is considered an optimum size for this age group. The size of the group can be increased for school-age children and adolescents, but usually it is limited to ten participants. Groups of six to ten are typical, with groups of adolescents tending to be larger than those for school-age children. Inexperienced therapists are urged to begin with a smaller and more manageable number of participants, although a minimum number is needed for the group process to occur.

Composition. Groups should attempt a balance in terms of gender. Although this is not always necessary, it becomes more important as children approach adolescence. A single boy or a single girl in a group may have difficulty establishing a sense of belonging and connection with other group members. Groups are most appropriate for children who have passed the initial period of shock and numbness following a loss. Adjusting to a group of strange peers may be threatening to the recently bereaved child. Younger children may also be experiencing a great deal of separation anxiety at this time. In order to effectively participate in a group, children need to be of an age and developmental level to have developed sufficient verbal skills for effective communication. By the age of three or four, most children have the social maturity to participate in a small group experience. Children and adolescents with extreme acting-out problems and hostility should be carefully screened prior to group participation, since their presence could be very disruptive for others. It should be stated, however, that many grieving children and adolescents have feelings of anger that can be constructively channeled as part of the group experience.

Structure. Groups for children and adolescents typically include activities that provide a common experience for all participants as well as avenues for individual self-expression. Activities should be planned to foster connection and communication among group members, but some less-structured time is also a critical component of weekly sessions. Planning and creativity on the part of the leader are keys to productive sessions. Generally, a team of co-leaders (ideally a male and a female) works best. In situations where one leader may have to remove a disruptive group member from the room, give an anxious child extra comfort, or assist someone with materials, the other leader can continue the work of the group.

Length of session and program. Older children and adolescents do well with one-hour sessions, allowing for more group processing as well as providing opportunity for full participation of all group members. With very young children, one-hour sessions may be too long to hold their attention effectively. Many therapists have found thirty to forty-five minutes to be an optimum amount of time for productive sessions for preschool and younger latency-age children.

Therapists tend to favor relatively short, time-limited groups with closed enrollments, which allow them to plan ahead, run the group for a specific period, end it, and then regroup (MacLennan, 1986). Six to eight weeks are common for the duration of these groups, with most meeting on a weekly basis. When only a few children or adolescents are in need of a bereavement group at any given time, the group can be run on an ongoing basis with open enrollment, beginning with two or three participants and adding others as the need arises.

Initial sessions. Since the initial session sets the tone for those to follow, an atmosphere of trust and sharing must be developed at the outset in which group members feel free to voice their concerns and support one another. Fear of the unknown is common among children as well as adolescents, and their first bereavement group experience is no exception. Masterman and Reams (1988) suggest that participants be told by parents that they are only required to attend the first session and that they need not return unless they wish to. Once children and adolescents realize that the group members are very much like themselves and that they will not be forced to say or do anything, their anxieties and fears are lessened. In fact, it is quite unusual for young clients to choose not to return after the first session. This meeting should include a discussion of why they think they are there and a sharing of thoughts and concerns about what might happen in the group. It is helpful if the therapist has met once individually with each child or adolescent before the first group meeting.

Confidentiality. Issues of confidentiality are important for therapists to consider at all times with all age groups. We agree with Masterman and Reams (1988) who recommend that school-age children and adolescents be told during the first group session that what they say will be confidential. Privacy is extremely important to adolescents and may become a major issue in therapy. Conversations with parents about the child's progress should offer the therapist's insights and observations but should not disclose specific statements made by the youngster. If the therapist feels a parent must be told about something that has occurred in the group, then the son or daughter should be informed first. Loss of trust and feelings of betrayal can severely damage the relationship of the child or adolescent with the group leader(s).

Confidentiality is less of an issue for young children than for older children, adolescents, or adults. Rarely do preschool children expect strict confidentiality in a clinical relationship, and it is usually unnecessary to meet the clinical objectives for a child's treatment (James, 1989). Therapists should, however, still maintain sensitivity to the child's sharing of difficult, and sometimes intimate, information. Specific statements made by the child should not be repeated unless it is deemed to be in the best interests of the child. Unusual reactions of preschoolers can be communicated in private to parents, which often helps them better interpret the child's reactions to the group or understand their child's symbolic play activities outside the sessions.

Termination.   For any group, termination is a difficult process. It evokes memories of previous endings and separations, and it is also a loss of special relationships developed within the group. Young clients may have an especially difficult time saying good-bye when therapy is over. Because of the high potential for stress, this transition needs to be handled with care and sensitivity.

The following segment of a group session for children aged nine to thirteen illustrates anger as well as other reactions to the anticipated termination of "their group." The group, which we have cited earlier in this chapter, was conducted at a child guidance center in an inner-city area having a high incidence of violence-related death (Vastola, Nierenberg, and Graham, 1986, pp. 87–88).

At the beginning of the session, the group discussion wandered without focus. The children seemed to be avoiding the work at hand.

LEADER: I noticed that no one has mentioned that next week is our last meeting.

DICK: It is? *(He looked stunned, as if he were hearing this for the first time.)*

GLORIA: *(Angrily)* Shoot.

LEADER: That's right. Next week is our last meeting.

DICK: So. What are you gonna do after next week?

LEADER: What do you think I might be doing?

DICK: Have another group.

LEADER: Maybe you feel you are going to be replaced?

TIM: Well, maybe.

DICK: With other people . . . let them get a chance . . . then after their weeks are up . . . then they're gonna be replaced . . . then after that, it goes on and on and on till everybody is dead.

137

LEADER: It sounds like that is what life has been like for you—many people replacing each other. *(Dick nodded.)* I am wondering if the others are feeling that they can be replaced. *(Tim started to name other children he felt should be in the group.)* I see your concern for the other children, but I'm wondering what the end of the group means for you.

TIM: It means I won't be coming here every week. That's what it means.

LEADER: How do you feel about that?

TIM: I don't really care.

LEADER: It sounds to me like you're both angry. *(No response.)* And I'm wondering if this ending of the group and the thoughts of people replacing one another reminds you of other people who have been replaced in your life? *(Silence.)*

TIM: *(After a few minutes)* Why should we tell you anything—if you really cared about it, you wouldn't end the group.

DICK: That's right! It's not fair.

LEADER: It seems many things have happened in your life that aren't fair.

GLORIA: That's right!

LEADER: Like people who you have loved, dying.

MATT: That's not fair! Other kids have their parents.

LEADER: And what is that like for you?

MATT: It makes me mad.

When terminating a therapeutic relationship with children and adolescents, it is important to prepare them in advance for this ending. They should be given the opportunity to express feelings surrounding the termination (such as anger and sadness), and these feelings should be validated and addressed. It is also important to review what they have gained from the group and remind them of how they can use this acquired skill, knowledge, and insight. Coupled with this should be discussions of the future and the difficult issues that they will continue to face. Youngsters, like adults, can benefit from a ritual or ceremony to conclude the series of sessions. When invited to participate in the planning, children and adolescents will often design a good-bye party that contains elements special and unique to them and their needs. Younger clients especially enjoy having a certificate of completion or some similar document given by the group leader(s) to take with them as a reminder of the experience.

Examples of groups

A program including children's groups for bereaved preschool and school-age children has been in operation in the state of Washington since 1982. Since that time more than 100 children have participated. Because of the nature of the program, which is organized under the auspices of the Widowed Information and Consultation Services, children participating in the program have typically experienced the death of a parent. The specific program content has been described in detail in an article by Masterman and Reams (1988), a summary of which is presented here as an example of the structure of an existing program.

Preschool group. The preschool group meets for eight, weekly one-hour sessions. Each session is divided into five segments: (1) a five-minute beginning discussion, (2) fifteen minutes of free play, (3) fifteen minutes of discussion based on therapeutic stories and role playing, (4) fifteen minutes of free play, and (5) ten minutes of discussion to conclude the session.

The initial discussion has a standard format and becomes an opening ritual the children can depend on. First, each child describes and shows off a toy he or she has brought from home. The children's attention is then drawn to the blackboard, where eight houses have been drawn to represent each session. The leader comments on the number of sessions left and mentions the common thread among the group participants—the fact that they have all suffered the death of a parent.

The two fifteen-minute play periods are useful for (1) providing the variation in format that young children need because of their limited attention spans, (2) encouraging the spontaneous expression of a wide range of emotions through play activities, (3) facilitating bonding among the children and with the group leader, and (4) giving permission to laugh and play. Toys used during the free-play period typically include a doctor's kit, paper and markers, a baby doll, and a doll house with family figures. Guided play is sometimes initiated with certain toys for certain children. Feelings and actions in the children's play are verbalized by the leader(s), and anger, guilt, and powerlessness are commonly observed.

The discussion period in the middle of each one-hour session focuses on the theme for the week. These themes include how the parent died, guilt over the child's perceived contribution to the parent's death, fear of oneself or the remaining parent dying, anger at the parent who died, what it is like where the deceased parent is now, getting along with siblings, memories and dreams, fear and sadness, and termination of the group. When introducing themes, the leaders keep in mind the preschoolers' attention span, vocabulary level, and general cognitive abilities. Therapeutic conclusions are stated in concrete terms and repeated often. The theme is typically introduced by the group leader with either stories or puppet plays. Unusual character names, varied voice tones, and clumsy character movements are used to maintain the attention of the preschool audience. Questions are used afterwards to highlight the relevance to the child's life ("Did you ever feel like if you act real good then maybe your dad would come back?").

The last segment provides closure for each weekly session and prepares the children for the completion of the eight-week program. Each week a different child crosses off one of the eight houses on the blackboard to indicate the end of another session. In addition, a concluding ritual is used each week, which involves all the children—typically, a cooperative game such as rolling a ball back and forth among the children sitting in a circle. The game emphasizes sharing and connection and is not too skill-based or rowdy.

School-age group.   The one-hour sessions are conducted weekly over a period of eight weeks. Each session follows the same general format: (1) a fifteen-minute discussion of the previous week's activities for group members, (2) a ten-minute discussion of the previously assigned homework, (3) twenty-five minutes of discussion on topics planned for the session, and (4) ten minutes spent in a closing game or activity. Although a leader's manual describes activities planned for each week, group leaders are encouraged to modify the structure to meet the needs of individual groups.

The first fifteen-minute period is devoted to discussing events of the previous week. (At the first session, the rules of the group are discussed and children are assured of confidentiality.) This activity gives the children a chance to talk about relatively nonthreatening topics and share varied aspects of their lives with their peers in the group.

During the next ten-minute portion, the group discusses the assigned homework activity for the previous week, which might be to draw a picture of their family or to write a letter or poem to the deceased parent. These assignments offer a concrete way to begin discussion of the session's topics and to introduce children to creative means of expressing their grief.

The third and longest portion of the session is devoted to discussions of difficult adjustment issues facing the children. The following is a typical schedule of activities and topics:

Week 1
- Play nonthreatening game.
- Discuss why they are in the group.
- Share thoughts and feelings about what will happen in the group.
- Review structure and topics for future sessions.

Week 2
- Have children describe parent who died, circumstances of the death, and how they heard about it. (The discussion is started by one of the leaders talking about his or her own loss experience. Children are encouraged to share only to the extent they feel comfortable.)

Week 3
- Examine thoughts and feelings about last rites, and discuss children's participation.
- Address children's fears and misunderstandings about death and funeral arrangements.

Week 4
- Discuss changes that have occurred in the family since the death, and their emotional impact. (These might include changes in financial status, in residence, in the personality of the surviving parent, or in distribution of household chores.)
- Identify problem areas and coping strategies.

Week 5
- Discuss bereavement reactions and individual perceptions of afterlife.

Week 6
- Discuss fears about the future, including fear of one's own death or that of surviving parent, and remarriage of that parent. (A story about a hypothetical stepfamily is read to stimulate discussion.)

Week 7
- Prepare for termination of group by discussion of feelings about it (negative and positive).
- Discuss alternative support systems.

Week 8
- Elicit verbal feedback for improving group.
- Encourage continued contact among group members by distributing phone lists.
- Have children write good-bye notes.
- Celebrate with a small party.

Following the twenty-five-minute discussion, the final ten-minute segment is spent in physical activity to allow a release of energy (folding and throwing paper airplanes, for example). It allows a socially appropriate expression of anger that may have surfaced in the preceding discussion and serves as a reward for the children's attentiveness during the discussion.

Adolescent group. DiMaio and Prunkl (1990) have described a grief support group they established for students (ages twelve through eighteen) in schools in Quincy, Illinois. The purpose of the group was to provide a safe, comfortable atmosphere for adolescents to express their feelings about their loss and to learn about the grief process. Prospective members, identified through questionnaires distributed in classes, were invited to attend a no-obligation informational session. (Twenty percent of the student body had lost someone close to them and were therefore eligible for the group.) Individual interviews were held with those interested in participating, and a family history as well as other pertinent information was gathered at this time.

142

Referred to as TIGERS (Teens in Grief: Educate, Rebuild, Support), the group met over eight weeks for forty- to fifty-minute sessions on the school premises. Each session was structured around a particular topic. These topics included the following:

1. *Grief and Mourning.* A discussion of the normal and varied manifestations of grief and aspects of mourning.
2. *What Am I Feeling?* An exploration of feelings experienced by the participants.
3. *Things Are Different at Home.* A discussion of how other family members are dealing with the loss and the changes that have taken place since the death.
4. *What Do I Need?* An exploration of the needs of each group member and what they feel will help them cope with the loss.
5. *How Do I Get What I Need?* A discussion of assertive, heathy ways for each adolescent to make his or her needs known to family members, friends, teachers.
6. *My Loved One Is Never Coming Back.* A presentation of mechanisms for present and future coping and a discussion of the finality of the loss.
7. *Where Are My Friends?* An examination of the important role of helpful and supportive peers at this time.
8. *I'm Going to Die Someday Too.* A healthy and appropriate exploration of feelings about their own mortality, usually activated by the loss of a loved one.

Evaluations of the program have confirmed its usefulness for this age group. DiMaio and Prunkl (1990) feel that such a group has an important place in a comprehensive student assistance program in the schools.

CHAPTER 7

Cultural Considerations in Grief Therapy

As a therapist in a university counseling center, you are asked to give a consultation to the foreign student office regarding a Nigerian student whose wife has committed suicide.

The director of a refugee relocation project refers a Haitian family to the county mental health center where you are working. Three family members have been murdered in what has been identified as a "hate crime."

You are a staff member at the psychiatric facility of a local hospital. While you are on emergency duty one weekend, an elderly Asian man is brought in by his family. They say he has stopped eating and has talked to no one since his wife died a month ago. His son became worried when his father suddenly got agitated and started shouting from the windows at cars.

You have been asked to lead a Hospice bereavement group for adolescents in an inner-city area. Most of the children come from black and Puerto Rican families.

Do any of these situations sound familiar to you? Depending on your background, you may have worked with many different ethnic groups or only a few. Regardless of your past experience, you are likely to be involved with a significant number of ethnically diverse clients in the future. Because of the changing composition of the U.S. population, therapists will need to be prepared to treat greater numbers of ethnic minorities in the coming decade (Saba, Karrer, and Hardy, 1989).

When speaking of the need for formal training in this area, Aponte (1990) has said: "Working with cultural and racial forces is not just a matter of personal or political belief. It is a question of effective therapy. The aim is not just to 'sensitize,' 'raise awareness,' or to be 'fair.' The goal is to learn how to diagnose, intervene, and relate with and through the richness and complexity of culture and race" (p. 3).

This chapter is intended to increase your competence in assessing cultural issues related to bereavement in a client-therapist relationship. We present primary aspects of therapy with reference to cultural issues that may emerge during the course of treatment. Our emphasis is on the diversity of responses to loss and the ways in which loss experiences are interpreted and processed within different cultural milieus. While we hope your knowledge of different groups will be increased, you should be aware that much diversity exists within any one cultural group. These variations may be regional, generational, socioeconomic, or idiosyncratic.

Client-Therapist Interactions

Culture is a major factor in the acceptance and utilization of mental health services. Ideas about health, illness, and healing are closely tied to the values of a culture and may limit the role that professional therapists are permitted to play. In many cultural groups, families are reluctant to accept outside help because it implies that somehow the family is incapable of taking care of itself. In Chinese culture, for example, receiving help from nonfamily members can result in "loss of face" *(tiu lien)*, a cause of great shame and embarrassment to Chinese families. Hispanics, who show strong feelings of obligation and interdependence in family relationships, tend to deemphasize the extent of family problems or may feel that they do not want to burden anyone outside the family (Ho, 1987). These issues need to be fully explored and their implications considered during the course of therapy.

Additional reasons for underutilization of mental health services by ethnic minorities include the following: (1) distrust of therapists, (2) cultural and social class differences between therapists and clients, (3) too few professionals who are bicultural, (4) overuse and misuse of physicians for emotional problems, (5) language barriers, and (6) lack of awareness of availability of professional services (Ho, 1987). Ethnic minorities may also consult folk healers or religious leaders rather than a psychotherapist. Some Hispanics still practice *curanderismo* (rural folk medicine), either instead of or simultaneously with mainstream mental and physical health services (Martinez, 1988).

On occasion, completely unexpected or idiosyncratic factors will elicit a negative response from ethnic minority clients and interfere with the provision of services. Recently, an adviser on a university campus told us that none of the Native American students whom he had referred to a particular counselor had kept their appointments. When he went to speak with her about this situation, the reason became obvious. Behind her desk hung a large weaving of an owl—the messenger of death among many Native American groups. Even such seemingly small matters as the decor of one's office can have a powerful effect on some clients.

Therapist-client roles

The therapist's theoretical stance typically dictates his or her role in therapy, ranging from that of reflective listener to that of strategist. While professional training supposedly exposes therapists to extremes along the active-passive continuum as it relates to the role of the therapist, one should not assume that all perspectives have been considered. Most training programs are, in fact, limited by the Western paradigm of therapist-client roles. In other cultures, the role of the participants in therapeutic relationships may be conceptualized in very different terms.

Among the Navaho, for example, the person seeking help often assumes a passive role during "treatment." An illustration of this would be instances in which a tribal singer conducts a "sing" in an effort to rid the individual of physical or psychological pain. (The Navaho have an elaborate array of ceremonial events called "sings," which may last from one to nine days and nights.) At the time of the ceremony, family, friends, and other well-wishers gather together to eat, dance, and pray for the patient.

During this ceremonial treatment, the client is relatively passive. All curative procedures and powers are seen to lie with the practitioner, who is the only one expected to have insights into the nature of the problem. This, of course, is at odds with traditional psychotherapy, which expects and values active involvement on the part of the client, self-expression, and introspective analysis. Part of the power of these ceremonial events comes from the hope-generating power of the singer's chants, the high expectations regarding the effectiveness of the treatment, and the support of the community during the ceremony. Traditional curing practices among Native Americans are community-based. Unlike traditional psychotherapy, the community and family participate in a very indirect way and are never expected to examine their role in the problem or to participate in an ongoing program to help the individual (Marsella and Pedersen, 1981).

What may appear as resistance on the part of a Native American client may simply be unfamiliarity and discomfort with the approach and the expectations of the therapist. The discrepancies between the role expectations that both the therapist and client bring to the session must be addressed before effective therapy can be undertaken.

Establishing trust and rapport

Since therapists uncover deep-seated thoughts and feelings only after a trusting relationship has been established, the dynamics of the initial meeting between therapist and client can be a powerful factor in setting the stage for the therapeutic relationship. Sometimes the client will not return after the first session, and the therapist is left wondering why.

The pacing of therapy and the time needed to establish trust and rapport varies from one cultural group to another. Marsella and Pedersen (1981), after reviewing a number of research findings, concluded that Hispanics tend to self-disclose less in therapy than do Anglos, a finding that holds true even when the therapist is Hispanic. Self-disclosure is influenced by the perceived acceptance by the therapist, and many clients continually assess whether or not they can trust this person. Boyd-Franklin (1989) has also pointed out that credibility among blacks is influenced by the professional's understanding and appreciation of cultural differences. Respect is not automatically granted because the therapist is in a position of authority and holds an advanced degree.

Closely associated with ethnicity is strength of family ties. In general, clients with strong multigenerational ties and allegiances may need more sessions allocated to trust building than those in which these are not present, since persons outside the extended family are sometimes viewed as strangers not to be trusted. Additionally, clients may withhold information and feelings out of fear of betraying their families.

Therapist-client communication

Cultural norms and customs can also affect client-therapist communication. Effective communication between therapist and client lays the foundation for productive work together, so misinterpretations and inaccurate perceptions can greatly interfere with the effectiveness of a treatment plan. Because of the diversity of cultural factors that can affect client-therapist interaction, possible communication barriers—differing languages, varied meanings of nonverbal cues, and disparate perspectives and use of space and time—need to be examined.

Language. Language serves as a primary system for expressing thoughts, feelings, and emotions. Many first-generation immigrants have extremely limited competency in English, but even when individuals are proficient in the language of the therapist, they may prefer to discuss emotionally laden topics in their primary language. Loss is a profound experience, and people often cannot find words (in any language) to express their sorrow. It can become even more difficult to express one's deepest thoughts in a secondary language, due in part to the energy drain brought on by the grief experience. Also, certain words, phrases, or concepts in one's primary language cannot always be adequately translated. For example, some cultures have few, if any, words for depression or shame, while other cultures have many words to reflect fine (and important) distinctions in these feeling states. Expressing nuances in feelings is important in the therapeutic process, and conveying these feelings is difficult (if not impossible) when someone is struggling with the language. In addition, some ethnic groups have a high regard for subtlety and indirectness, whereas others value directness and confrontation, which can add to the confusion in therapist-client communication.

Certain cultures depend much more on the context of language and implied meaning than do others. The Japanese, for example, have dozens of ways of implying "no," but they rarely say the word "no," so one should understand that a "maybe" often means "no." The Japanese also use the sound "hai" a lot, literally meaning "yes" but usually indicating understanding rather than agreement. Sometimes gestures substitute for words or concepts. Samovar and Porter (1991) give the following example: "The nonverbal symbol for suicide varies among cultures. In the United States it is usually a finger pointed at the temple or drawn across the throat. In Japan, it is a hand thrust onto the stomach, and in New Guinea it is a hand placed on the neck" (p. 18).

There are also structural differences in the ways different groups converse. For example, the nearly universal question-answer sequence is not found in some African societies, where information is viewed as precious and is not readily given away. And Arabs, among other groups, have a half-hour chat before getting down to business in formal settings (Samovar and Porter, 1991), so clients from these cultures may feel uncomfortable with the "format" of therapy sessions as they are typically practiced in the United States.

Obviously, therapist proficiency in other languages and customs is desirable, but as an alternative, requesting that someone—a respected person in the client's community or a paraprofessional—serve as a translator during the sessions is a viable option. The therapist should also recognize his or her own limitations and, when appropriate, refer the client to another therapist who has more knowledge of the client's language and culture.

Nonverbal communication. In therapy, communication through nonverbal means is equally important. In fact, it has been estimated that in two-person conversations, words communicate only about 35 percent of the social meaning of a situation and nonverbal elements convey more than 65 percent of the meaning (Samovar and Porter, 1991). Clinicians, in particular, have been trained to respond to nonverbal cues, relying on them to detect feeling states and to determine dissonance between what is said and what is felt by the client.

Culture is a main contributor to how we send, receive, and respond to these nonverbal signals, with each of us basing his or her interpretation of behavior on what we have learned within the context of our own culture. When therapist and client are from different backgrounds, there is a greater likelihood of misinterpretation. One study found that Japanese professionals working in a long-term-care facility perceived Japanese patients as being depressed, while Caucasian staff, observing the same patients, described them as merely "quiet" (Lister, 1977). A Caucasian may also interpret an Asian-American's calmness after a loss as denial if it occurs soon after bereavement, but another Asian may view it simply as the acceptance of death. As these examples illustrate, cultural differences can interfere with the therapist's full understanding and appreciation of the inner experience of the individual.

No expression, position, or movement has the same meaning in every culture. Facial expressions, eye contact, body movements and positioning, posture, and gestures can convey quite different meanings for different cultural groups. Eye contact in some cultures implies good communication skills, but in others, such as certain Native American groups, it is a sign of disrespect if the person in the path of your gaze is an elder or authority figure. Anglos working in mental health facilities on reservations could interpret avoidance of eye contact among clients as an indication of inattention or lack of interest in therapy. Or they may assume that the client does not understand them and may persistently rephrase or repeat sentences. Among Saudi Arabians, both the speaker and the listener engage in mutual eye contact almost continuously, which could be seen as disrespectful, threatening, or insulting to people from other cultures.

Unfamiliar gestures may also confuse the therapist. Saudi Arabians place a forefinger on the side of their nose to indicate dislike of an idea; disagreement in Greece and southern Italy is indicated by an upward head toss. Whereas widened eyes expresses anger and disgust among the Chinese, it signifies a request for help for Hispanics and a challenge among the French. Different cultural rules also dictate when one is permitted to laugh, cry, and so on. Japanese cultural rules, for example, generally prohibit negative facial expressions (Samovar and Porter, 1991).

Silence is one aspect of interpersonal communication that has received little attention. When a client uses silence in therapy, the therapist must know how to interpret it accurately. Ishii and Bruneau (1991) caution that the intercultural implications of this behavior are diverse and can vary markedly from one culture to the next. It can be interpreted as coldness, aloofness, defiance, approval, consent, respect, awkwardness, embarrassment, or humility. For Northern European and North American societies, for example, silence is viewed as dark, negative, and discomforting. Even flashes of silence are often filled with some activity. In these cultures, it is much more acceptable to have an absence of conversation in rituals and ceremonies than in interpersonal communication. Other cultural groups, especially those from the Far East, are biased toward lengthy silences. Individuals from these groups value and accept quiet intervals during discourse. In fact, deep and long silences are viewed as contemplative and positive.

Perceptions of space and time.   Two of the most fundamental differences in intercultural communication involve space and time, elements that are not only important components of the structure of therapy, but that may also have relevance for the expectations regarding successful resolution of grief. Cultures differ substantially in their use of personal space, the interpersonal distances they maintain, and their regard for personal boundaries. When talking to someone with a Latin American or Arabic background, for example, be prepared for them to sit physically closer to you than you may feel comfortable with if you are Anglo. Rather than viewing their behavior as overbearing or an inappropriate violation of your personal space, try to place it in the context of their familiar patterns of behavior. If you are working with an extended family, relatives sitting closely together on a couch may have many different meanings, and a cultural explanation should always be considered. In some cultures, bodily contact (apart from greetings and partings) is confined to family members, and contact outside of this context can be considered a source of much anxiety. Physical orientation is also culturally influenced. North Americans prefer to sit facing each other at right angles, whereas Chinese prefer and feel more comfortable in a side-to-side arrangement (Samovar and Porter, 1991).

Different cultural concepts of time affect therapy in numerous ways—promptness for sessions, perception of the segments allocated for each session, and acceptance of the appropriate duration of the course of therapy. Many segments of American society are exceedingly time bound, breaking each day into discrete units and allocating them for specific purposes. This linear, time-guarding approach is very foreign to some other cultures. For example, among the Hopi Indians the period that is devoted to a task or event is determined by the time that is needed (which can't be predetermined) rather than settling on a time slot (say, fifty minutes) beforehand. In terms of arriving for sessions on time, how late is "late"? Among the British and most North Americans, five minutes late would be acceptable for a professional appointment, but not fifteen and never thirty minutes. Other cultures without such an emphasis on time may find these parameters extremely rigid and inflexible.

Issues Related to Diagnosis and Treatment

Diagnosis and treatment decisions are crucial to the success of any therapeutic endeavor. Unfortunately, even the best-trained professionals are often unaware of the complex ways in which cultural factors can influence mental and physical health. Even our accepted definitions of "health" are to some extent culturally determined.

Cultural factors affecting diagnosis

Therapists must be cautious in concluding that a particular client is "unhealthy" or "abnormal" when, in fact, the client may be responding in a way that is quite normal for his or her culture. Westermeyer (1987) has emphasized that "understanding the sociocultural milieu in which the patient lives and functions is crucial for distinguishing psychopathology from culture-bound beliefs or behavior" (p. 60).

Since culture influences the overt expression of feelings and the manifestation of emotional pain and discomfort, the ways of behaving publicly during the period of mourning are quite varied. In judging the appropriateness (and potential pathology) of grief reactions, the therapist must take these cultural differences into account, since the presence and intensity of grief reactions have a cultural component. In Japan, mourners smile so that others will not be burdened. Puerto Ricans (especially females), on the other hand, are prone to demonstrative displays of intense, convulsive hysteria (known as *ataques*) at times of loss. The Japanese value "saving face" at all costs and may feel intense guilt and shame if they show strong emotions or feel out of control in public, whereas Hispanic cultures value freedom of emotional expression; therefore, therapists should never urge clients to express or inhibit grief in a manner that is alien to them.

Cultural factors can also affect patterns of symptomatology, which could result in misdiagnoses. For example, one recent study (Oltjenbruns, 1989) found that bereaved Mexican-American college students, when compared to their Anglo-American counterparts, were more likely to express their emotions openly. They were also more likely to have physical symptoms associated with grief, such as gastrointestinal problems. It is possible for a therapist with little understanding of Hispanic culture to feel that the client is "out of control" and perhaps suggest a psychiatric consultation unnecessarily. In addition, therapists might not see this clientele as often because these bereaved individuals may have focused on their physical problems and sought services from a physician instead. A close working relationship with health care professionals in the community is important in order to acquaint them with circumstances in which referral for grief therapy might be appropriate.

Interpretation of the loss

Certainly when working with any individual, it is important to assess the meaning of the particular loss and understand its added meaning because of what it symbolizes to the person. Cultural factors can affect which relationships are mourned and how they are mourned. In some matrilineal societies in Africa, for example, a person is only a relative of the mother's kin and is not thought to be related to the father's kinship group. Consequently, the death of one's father or a member of his family would not be seen as a personal loss, and to mourn that death would be viewed as inappropriate in that society (Kamerman, 1988).

In traditional Ireland, responses to death can vary greatly depending on the type of death. According to Gaines (1986):

Critical to the traditional Irish response to the trauma of death is the assessment of the appropriateness of the age of the deceased. If death comes to someone who is considered young, it is a great tragedy. As such, it is a time of great mourning and "keening" (Irish wailing). However, if an older person dies, one who in the cultural conception has lived a full life (married, farmed, had children and grandchildren), then death and the wake will be occasions not for sorrow or keening, but for joy and laughter. Thus, death *per se* has no constant meaning. Rather, depending on the social state of the individual in question, old or young, the response may be sorrowful or joyous. (p. 7)

Appropriate use of techniques and interventions

Cultural norms and customs pertaining to status, family patterns, and values influence the choice of therapeutic techniques. Many of the contemporary techniques used by American therapists are derived from Western cultures that emphasize individuality, independence, directness, and verbal expression. Many other cultures, in contrast, value group identity, deference to authority, indirectness, and intuition. The following case illustrates the inappropriate application of an intervention technique.

Mei-ling, a foreign student from Taiwan, came to the counseling center at the midwestern university she attended, reporting that she often felt depressed and anxious and that she thought of home much of the time since arriving in the United States six weeks earlier. Recently, she was even having trouble sleeping and had lost her appetite. After a brief discussion, the therapist discovered that Mei-ling's father had died about two months earlier after a long illness. Further probing and questioning by the therapist revealed that Mei-ling had not talked to her father much about his illness and impending death. It is considered inappropriate in Chinese culture to express your feelings to the dying.

The therapist immediately assumed that Mei-ling had some un-resolved issues surrounding her father's death and her unexpressed feelings toward him. She proceeded to apply the Gestalt empty-chair technique in which the client is asked to imagine an individual (in this case Mei-ling's father) sitting in a chair in front of her. Mei-ling's therapist asked her to face him directly and share her deepest feelings. Showing great discomfort with this request, Mei-ling politely de-clined. After much prodding by the therapist, Mei-ling finally con-sented, but got increasingly anxious as she attempted to express her feelings in this way. At the end of the session, the therapist told Mei-ling that she had a great deal more work to do in this area and scheduled an appointment for the following week. Mei-ling did not return for the appointment and made no further contacts with the therapist.

First, the therapist failed to do a complete assessment of this client. It would certainly have been important to assess how much the cultural adjustment contributed to the symptomology of someone who had so recently relocated to a foreign country. Also, other undisclosed factors may have been relevant. Not only did the therapist proceed too quickly after discovering Mei-ling's recent loss, but she failed to consider important cultural variables when choosing to use the empty-chair technique. Chinese families are traditionally patriarchal, with communication and authority belonging to males and older adults. Filial piety, or respect and reverence for one's elders, is still adhered to by younger members of Chinese society. It is considered extremely rude and disrespectful to talk back to one's parents and to express anger or hostility. Guilt and shame are principal techniques used to control the behavior of family members and to socialize them into this tradition. What must Mei-ling have been feeling as she left the therapist's office? In what ways could the session have been counterproductive or even harmful? What would have been a more valid approach of working with this student and helping her cope with her depression and anxiety?

Conflicts in values can also be seen when techniques used by the therapist are in opposition to the time orientation of the client population. Whereas middle-class clients tend to have a future orientation, low-income clients are more likely to emphasize the here-and-now. Delgado (1981) recommends that therapists working with low-income Hispanics use an active approach with short-term, concrete solutions to problems rather than a long-term approach emphasizing insight and attitude change.

Recognition of customs and traditions

Traditions surrounding death and bereavement are perhaps the most conservative and resistant to change of any cultural or subcultural traditions because they are so deeply rooted in the values of the cultural group. Therapists would do well to learn about the customs of their clients and apply that knowledge in the overall treatment plan. Cultural traditions and rituals can help give meaning to the loss and aid in resolution of grief.

Tradition for Native Americans, for example, serves as a guide, an anchor, passed down by example and through tribal legends. Many Native American groups view tribal legends as offering great opportunities for learning, since knowledge is thought to come from the stories of the past. These stories are often recalled at times when wisdom and advice are sought. Dancing is another important ritual among many Native American groups. While dancing for Anglos is an expression of pleasure, dancing for Native Americans is an expression of their religion. For many participants, it provides (1) a strong sense of identity and pride in their culture, (2) a sense of belonging to a community, (3) a reaffirmation of social bonds, and (4) a connection with powerful mystical forces in the universe. In addition, it can have a very cathartic effect leading to the ventilation of intense feelings.

One of the first questions asked of a bereaved client should relate to customary rituals used to honor the deceased. In the Japanese culture, the deceased become revered ancestors whose memory is preserved by an altar in their home. In Anglo-American culture, having a shrine in the living room devoted to the deceased and bowing to it each day would be viewed as pathological and a sign of prolonged mourning. Some cultures focus more on the here-and-now or are future-oriented, whereas others pay special homage to the past. These time orientations can also affect the period of mourning typically observed. Navahos try to forget the dead as soon as possible, and they are expected to return to ordinary life after three or four days. In contrast, traditional Chinese families observe a forty-nine-day period of formal mourning. This background information from a broad cultural perspective is important for differentiating healthy from unhealthy responses to the loss.

Other related questions pertain to the client's ability to carry out these familiar traditions in a foreign environment. Does the American work system allow only three days for mourning instead of the number of days the client's culture calls for to complete all duty-bound rituals? Do American urban laws deny citizens of foreign descent the traditional manner of burying their dead? Are there certain rituals they did not get to participate in that they feel are essential for the deceased soul "to rest"? As the therapist explores these questions and others, the focus should be on the implications for the client. Has cultural incongruence in values and customs created some issues that will interfere with the successful resolution of grief? The therapist must explore the meaning behind the rituals and customs of which the bereaved was deprived and work with the client to find other ways to address the needs left unmet.

It should be remembered that what is a sacred tradition to one person may seem trivial or even disrespectful to another. Sensitivity to the meaning and power of cultural ritual requires placing our own judgments and reactions in perspective. As we have seen, lack of appreciation of these aspects of culture can result in inappropriate interpretations and actions on the part of the therapist.

Appreciation and respect for belief systems

Effective therapy requires that therapists acknowledge and incorporate the client's belief system into their interventions. In all cultures, the meaning of loss is interpreted within a broader scheme of beliefs and attitudes, often referred to as a "world view," which encompasses basic beliefs regarding illness, death, and healing. Lewis (1985) emphasizes, for example, that when working with Native Americans "one must first recognize the cultural concept of healing power. To the Native American, healing power is evident in all of nature. Nature, the life process itself, offers people numerous opportunities for healing power" (p. 458). Lewis offers two case studies that illustrate this concept. The first one demonstrates how a therapist can use a "power-revealing event" that occurs in the course of therapy; the second shows the importance of accepting a Native American client's prophetic interpretation of a dream.

> Joe Nighthawk, a twenty-one-year-old full-blooded Cherokee, severely depressed, came to the therapist very excited because a nighthawk (sacred bird to the Cherokee) had been found injured in his backyard and he had nursed it back to health. To him this was indeed a good omen. Instead of passing it off as pure superstition, the therapist stated that he was pleased because, with the appearance of the omen, improvement in all areas of life might occur and that maybe this sign meant he should use the positive forces and strength in his life to cope. The patient appeared very encouraged and elated as he left the office. (p. 459)

A Native American woman who was very depressed over her husband's death reported a dream in which her husband came back to her as a bird. In her husband's voice, the bird said that he was in a better place now and was waiting for her to join him. He said that she must be strong for the grandchildren. After talking about the dream, the woman seemed happier and relieved about her future. The therapist expressed confidence in the message of the dream, but did not attempt to interpret it. This type of situation needs no interpretation to a Native American—its meaning is quite clear. (p. 460)

Dreams and visions are important sources of information to the Native American, and discrediting these perceived "power sources" as mere superstitions shows a lack of appreciation for the person's rich cultural heritage and system of beliefs. To do so might actually create conflicts within the client instead of reducing suffering.

In situations involving severe illness or recent death, many people turn to religious practices for solace and hope. These practices vary not only by religion but by culture. Among Mexican-Americans, common practices are promise making, offerings to the church (such as medals, amulets, or candles), and prayer offerings and can include promises involving deprivation of some physical comfort (Falicov, 1982).

Using existing resources and social supports

Family. The families of clients—both nuclear and extended—can have a potent effect on the dynamics and outcomes of interventions. Clinicians of all orientations will want to acknowledge the importance of the family, which can provide valuable assistance during treatment. Martinez (1988) has discussed the extensive kin network of Mexican-Americans, pointing out that ties to the family in this culture tend to be strong and complex. For example, a *compadrazgo* (godparent) system exists in which close friends of parents agree to be supportive and helpful to a child, sometimes functioning as an extra set of parents. Because of the emphasis on family, Mexican-Americans very often turn to family members during a time of stress.

Use of a supportive family network can help clients tolerate emotional discomfort and minimize negative outcomes of a loss. Therapists should be aware of the strength and extent of the family system and use it as a resource in therapy. (Natural helping systems have generally been neglected by therapists.) While kinship can buffer the impact of certain stressors, the responsibilities and emotional involvement with a large number of family members can occasionally present an additional source of stress. Therapists should be alert to this fact and not assume that close family networks are always supportive.

Religion.   Oftentimes attitudes about death are deeply rooted in religious beliefs prevalent within a particular culture, giving it meaning and making the emotional pain of loss bearable. Religion usually provides a belief system regarding life after death and the hope for reunification. The bereaved may also find great solace in the rituals associated with their faith, especially those used at times of death. At a time in our society when many of our traditions regarding mourning have disappeared, religious institutions can provide some structure as a main purveyor of ritual. In religions having congregational worship, it can provide a source of ongoing community support after the loss of a loved one. And churches can often mobilize quickly and offer assistance to families in times of crisis.

Boyd-Franklin (1989) has emphasized that therapists, when assessing strengths and coping skills of black families, must be sensitive to the central role that religion and spirituality play in the lives of many blacks. "Training in the mental health fields largely ignores the role of spirituality and religious beliefs in the development of the psyche and in its impact on family life. In the treatment of black families, this oversight is a serious one" (p. 78). Kalish and Reynolds (1976) found that black families were almost twice as likely as other ethnic groups to identify religion as the main influence on their attitudes toward death. They will often frame their loss in the context of religion ("God gives you no more than you can carry," "The Lord will hear my prayers and heal me"). Unless these beliefs are respected by the therapist, clients are likely to feel alienated. For many, the church functions essentially as a type of extended family, and the minister is often contacted in times of emotional distress. Boyd-Franklin recommends that therapists working with black families use ministers as a resource.

Resolution of Grief and Termination of Therapy

Although issues pertaining to termination have been discussed earlier in the book, it is important to consider ways in which cultural factors may affect evaluation of progress and, thus, termination decisions. In addition to assessing and monitoring inner processes, the therapist also looks for cues from the client's behavior that will reflect the person's progression through the phases of grief work, but different cultures send different signals about what is appropriate or inappropriate behavior in the bereaved. If the therapist makes assumptions based solely on his or her own cultural experience, the behavior of the client may be misread. Because resolution of grief is affected by societal expectations, the therapist must recognize the messages coming from the client's subculture in order to interpret accurately what is being said and done.

Kalish and Reynolds (1976), in their comparison of ethnic groups, found that 39 percent of black respondents thought it was unimportant to wait to return to work after a death, while another 39 percent said they would wait one day to one week. In contrast, a third of the Japanese-Americans would prefer to wait a month or longer. Among Mexican-Americans, about a third thought it was proper to wear black for at least six months, while blacks placed less emphasis on this aspect of mourning behavior and expected that if it did occur, it would be of shorter duration. Mexican-Americans and Japanese-Americans expressed more conservative attitudes toward remarriage and dating following loss of a spouse than did blacks and Anglos. Style of clothing, use of cosmetics or jewelry, and changes in social patterns can be more a reflection of social expectations than a statement about the client's psychological functioning and emotional well-being. The therapist should be cognizant of this when identifying milestones in bereavement.

Culture may play a significant role in client perceptions and reactions at the actual time of termination. Ho (1987) has noted that Hispanic-American clients place such great value on interpersonal relationships and family ties that the process of termination is foreign to them. He thinks it is important that the therapist be prepared for a range of reactions. Because termination can be perceived as a significant loss by many clients, this final phase of therapy must be handled with sensitivity.

Cultural Change and Effects on Grief

The history of particular ethnic or cultural groups can have a profound effect on their experience of loss, so therapists ought to have some knowledge of recent cultural history that might have direct implications for their client. These factors can provide a greater understanding of the social and cultural supports available to the individual.

Refugees: Displaced grievers

Refugees who come to the United States typically have had significant losses. Currently, Southeast Asians form a large number of such refugees, many of whom have fled their homeland during a time of military conflict. Leaving treasured belongings and loved ones behind, they and their families were traumatically uprooted from all that was familiar to them. Many had friends and relatives who were killed shortly before their departure; others were separated from family members during their evacuation, and their whereabouts remain unknown. The rush to escape a life-threatening situation often did not allow for adequate mourning of their losses. Uncertainty regarding their own survival and well-being added to their personal chaos and turmoil. Upon arriving in the United States, refugees not only experienced culture shock, but many experienced a shift in identity as well. Middle-class professionals often found themselves poverty-stricken and forced to do menial labor in order to support themselves and their families. Their entire lifestyle and sense of self were disrupted.

When refugees experience the death of a loved one after arriving in their new country, they may find it difficult to engage in their traditional mourning practices. This is illustrated by Reade (1981) in his report of a Chinese woman from Vietnam who lost her husband about a year after arriving in Britain and was relocated to an area far from other Vietnamese refugees. She and her family had spent the previous nine months in a refugee camp in Hong Kong. The following summary of her experience reveals the additional difficulties that added to her bereavement distress.

Mui's husband died quite suddenly of viral pneumonia, leaving her with five young children. She felt guilty and remorseful for not getting medical help for him earlier, but the strangeness of the host country made her timid and confused about where to go for assistance. Following his death, the conflicts in cultures became immediately apparent. The imagery of death in Britain is symbolized by men in black coats and black limousines; in China, white symbolizes death and mourning.

In Chinese culture, funeral rituals are intended both to help the spirit of the deceased and to protect the living from the ill omen of the funeral itself. Mui wanted to prepare the body for burial and dress her husband in his finest clothes, but the Western custom of using professionals for this task did not permit her involvement. Refugee workers also discouraged it because of the condition of the body. An autopsy had been performed (a procedure required by law if a death is unattended). Eventually, the family was permitted to visit the body in the mortuary and perform a religious ceremony involving rice and chicken, during which time a coin was placed in the mouth of the deceased to help his spirit on its way. Unfortunately, rigor mortis had set in, and the funeral director had to pry the deceased's mouth open in order to insert the coin.

Shortly thereafter, the body was flown to a location some 400 miles away to be buried near Mui's closest living relatives. The procedure raised some questions in Mui's mind about whether her husband's spirit might lose contact with his body. According to her belief system, the spirit is expected to return several days after death. Since no one was at the family home and the corpse was far away, there was concern that his spirit might wander aimlessly. Once reunited with the body, Mui and her relatives took photographs of the reopened casket and close-ups of her deceased husband's face.

Additional conflict arose when choosing the gravesite. Mui's elderly mother wanted the grave to be dug pointing south. The cemetery superintendent said that it could only point southeast in order to conform to the alignment of the other plots. The family also requested land that had been consecrated but were told that only unconsecrated ground was available. Despite their pleading, their wishes were denied. Adding to their distress, they discovered that the high cost of the burial did not include a headstone. While they felt the grave should not remain unmarked, they were told by the superintendent that wooden crosses and concrete headstones were not allowed. According to cemetery rules, they could make their own headstone but only if marble or Portland stone were used. The family said good-bye to their loved one, unsure if his soul and body had found a proper resting place.

The widow still faced other obstacles after the burial. Initially, her brothers (one fearing for his pregnant wife) would not allow Mui and her children to live with them since, in their culture, persons associated with death transmit bad fortune. Eventually, the blessing of a Buddhist monk influenced one brother to relent. Her adjustment continued. She survived the Western world of coroners, death certificates, cemetery regulations, wills, probate, and widow's pension, only to find herself unemployed, with limited English skills, in a strange land with a climate to which she was unaccustomed, and unable to get familiar foods.

In Mui's case, a vital rite of passage had been compromised. What are some possible repercussions for this person? What alternatives were available given the situation? As a therapist, how might you have provided assistance?

While the pervasive loss described in this section can apply to all refugees, it must be remembered that each group has unique experiences and sometimes quite different cultural heritages. For example, Southeast Asian refugees comprise at least five distinct groups: Vietnamese, Kampucheans, Hmong, Lao, and Lao-Theung. Cross-cutting these, with their different geographical origins, are the ethnic Chinese. Consequently, vast disparities can exist in the social and religious practices among the refugees from Southeast Asia. The Vietnamese and Chinese-Vietnamese, for instance, may be Mahayana or Theravada Buddhist or Catholic; the Hmong and other hill tribes are usually animist. Each belief system has its own rituals associated with death, therefore therapists working with refugees need to be alert to these important differences, understand their implications, and be sensitive to potential points of conflict with the beliefs and rituals of the host country (Eisenbruch, 1984).

Issues of acculturation

In a pluralistic society such as the United States, clearly defined and accepted cultural norms and expectations can become blurred. First-generation immigrants may face a particularly difficult period of grief because they do not have the traditional resources for carrying out culturally expected bereavement practices. At the same time, they do not feel comfortable engaging in the mainstream bereavement practices of their new country (Kleinman, Kaplan, and Weiss, 1984). For example, most Issei (first-generation Japanese-Americans) came to the United States and Canada with the expectation of accumulating assets and then returning to Japan, but instead their fate has been to grow old and face death in a milieu that is much at variance with their values.

Compounding this situation is the tendency toward acculturation among future generations of Japanese. The Issei, having raised their families in Western society, find that their children and grandchildren (the Nisei and Sansei, respectively) are often more comfortable speaking English than Japanese, are unfamiliar with some sacred Japanese traditions, and are in some cases more likely to identify with the American culture than with the Japanese. Many elders justifiably fear that the relevance of traditional values is likely to be reduced as a result of acculturation and assimilation into the melting pot of American society.

Studies of ethnic identity among Japanese-Americans have in fact suggested a trend away from traditional Japanese values with each successive generation (Matsumoto, Meredith, and Masuda, 1970); therefore, when older Japanese-Americans experience a loss, they not only find themselves without their traditions related to loss, they are also surrounded by family members who may not understand the importance of these traditions for the grieving individual. When members of the same family have different values because of societal pressures toward acculturation, the potential for conflict and misunderstanding increases. Family members, instead of serving as a primary support, may exacerbate the feelings of loss and abandonment for the bereaved.

Acculturation can also occur as a result of government policies, in addition to geographic mobility and social change. For Native Americans living on reservations, many of the traditional ways continue to be maintained today. Most Native Americans in contemporary society, however, live in cities, separated from their traditional helping systems and rituals for handling times of transition. These people, for the most part, cannot be thought of as having been truly acculturated, since they still retain their sense of cultural identity as Navaho, Hopi, et cetera. However, displaced from the traditions associated with their ethnic heritage and their extensive kin network, they have nothing to replace them with and often exist in a vacuum of cultural and social support. London and DeVore (1988) charge the U.S. government with diminishing the influence of Native American culture on its people through policies aimed at assimilating Native American populations. As a result, the traditional protection and support offered by the larger group have been lost in some instances, posing special challenges to therapists.

Socioeconomic Influences

Therapists must consider not only the cultural context of grief, but the social and economic contexts as well—factors often linked with ethnicity. In American society, for example, ethnic minorities have had to contend with prejudice and discrimination and have not equitably shared in the benefits of adequate employment, education, and health care (Saba, Karrer, and Hardy, 1989).

McCubbin and Patterson (1983) have discussed the key variables that affect a person's ability to recover from a crisis: (1) concurrent stressors, (2) available resources, and (3) the interpretation of the crisis event. While cultural beliefs and traditional sources of strength and support can serve as resources and positively influence one's adjustment following a loss, the realities in some ethnic minority families work against a positive outcome. Additional burdens imposed by low incomes, restricted access to social and economic opportunities, prejudice, and inadequate health care can increase one's vulnerability at a time of loss. As we have learned, intense grief involves physical manifestations that can put one's health at risk, and in situations where well-being is already jeopardized by inadequate nutrition and living conditions, the physical and psychological health of the bereaved may be even further compromised.

The Therapist's Cultural Background

It is easy when discussing cultural differences to think of exotic examples from faraway places and to exclude one's own background from consideration. There is a tendency to view one's own socialization as reflecting the "norm" for appropriate behavior, especially if one is from a mainstream culture. In fact, we all come from a specific cultural environment, and it is this cultural context that shapes our own views toward loss, the expression of feelings, and the process of change—all critical elements in therapy. Culture affects every client, not just those of a different color or those who speak a different language, and our own cultural background influences our interactions with clients. Therapists will be able to detect the subtleties in cultural influences only after they have challenged some of their own beliefs and gained some insight into the origins of those beliefs. Sue and Sue (1990) describe the well-functioning practitioner as one who has moved from being culturally unaware to being aware and sensitive to his or her own cultural heritage and to valuing and respecting differences.

McGoldrick and Rohrbaugh (1987) surveyed mental health professionals in an effort to demonstrate empirically cultural differences in attitudes among therapists. Clinicians who completed the questionnaires identified three of their four biological grandparents as having the same ethnic affiliation. The researchers found that there was a common set of values and expected behaviors among individuals reared in particular ethnic groups, and that these shared attitudes, beliefs, and patterns of relating have important implications for the ways that different ethnic groups cope with grief issues. To illustrate, McGoldrick and Rohrbaugh found that therapists of Jewish heritage generally agreed that in their families talking about one's problems was considered the best way to cope with them and that suffering was to be expressed and shared. Also, children were encouraged to discuss and give their opinions about family problems. In contrast, Anglo therapists were more likely to say their families valued self-control, avoided conflict, and believed that suffering was to be endured in silence.

It is interesting to speculate how a WASP (White Anglo-Saxon Protestant) therapist might react in a situation in which a large Jewish family requests therapy following a death. Would the therapist include the children in any therapy sessions? If so, how actively would they be involved and what kinds of questions would be directed toward them? How might the therapist react to an outpouring of emotion from the adult clients? How could the therapist's values regarding "appropriate behavior" affect the process of therapy?

Consider your own ethnic background. What potential conflicts and misunderstandings might occur if you were seeing a client from a different ethnic group? If you were the client, what aspects from your own background might not be completely understood and appreciated by a therapist from a different cultural heritage?

In summary, the following guidelines are recommended when working with culturally diverse populations:

1. Recognize the cultural influences in your own life and how they affect your work as a therapist.
2. Acknowledge your own limitations when working with culturally diverse groups. Be creative and explore alternatives for overcoming these limitations.
3. Be open to learning about cultural traditions and beliefs. Identify strengths from the person's cultural background and use them as resources in the process of therapy.
4. Appreciate the history and experiences of different cultural groups in the United States (for example, refugees, first-generation immigrants) and identify areas of greatest vulnerability and strength.
5. Accept the wide variation in expressions of grief and ways of coping with loss.
6. Recognize that loss is a universal experience, having a profound effect on our lives regardless of our differences in language, lifestyle, and patterns of relating.

As part of the process of working with individuals and families from diverse cultures, you will become increasingly aware of your own stereotypes, biases, and "blind spots." If you are open, you will also have the opportunity to learn from other cultural traditions and gain additional perspectives on grief and loss. Acknowledging and appreciating cultural diversity and its far-reaching implications can be an enriching experience.

CHAPTER 8

Looking Inward: Therapist's Self-Examination

WORKING as a therapist in the area of grief and loss requires an awareness of yourself and your own issues. Who you are as a person affects the way you interact with clients and how you conduct therapy. With issues related to death, the therapist-client dynamics are even more complex than with other types of therapy. Issues surrounding grief and loss are highly emotional, touching our deepest fears as human beings. As a therapist in this field, you will come face-to-face with your own mortality and your own fears of dying and losing loved ones. If you are not in touch with your own issues in this area, your work with clients can be seriously compromised. On the other hand, an awareness of your own vulnerabilities and influences can have a positive effect on your work with clients and allow you to minimize the possible adverse effects. Three areas we ask you to explore are (1) your background related to death, (2) your current personal issues related to grief and loss, and (3) your motivation as a helper.

Your Background Related to Death

Therapists all come from different backgrounds, grow up within unique families, and are influenced by a cultural context. Some are familiar with loss; they have been touched by it often. Others have not. How your family dealt with its losses has affected your experience of loss and your perceptions of it. How well you are able to accept loss will affect your ability to work with grieving clients. Therefore, self-examination and ongoing attention to personal issues surrounding death and other types of loss is critical if you are going to work in the field of grief therapy.

To increase your awareness of your experiences with death and the ways in which your attitudes have been influenced, consider the following questions:

1. What was your first encounter with death? Recall your feelings and needs at the time. How did others respond to those feelings and needs? What is your most vivid image associated with this first loss experience?
2. How was the topic of death dealt with in your family? Was it ignored? Was it considered taboo? Was it discussed openly and matter-of-factly?
3. Can you remember the first funeral that you attended? How were you prepared for this experience? What do you remember about it? What feelings did you have? How was the funeral and your response influenced by religion and culture?
4. What significant losses have you had? Which one was the most painful and why? In what ways has this affected your life? In what ways, if any, has this affected the way you do therapy?

Your Current Issues Related to Grief and Loss

In addition to your background, your work as a grief therapist will be influenced by your current level of psychological growth. Just because we are therapists does not mean we have examined and resolved all of our own issues. Most of us continue to work on old patterns that influence our lives, and as evolving human beings, we constantly encounter new issues as we grow and change. We are also expanding our perspectives on grief and loss as we work with our clients and experience more of our own losses. Your personal perspectives and reactions can, to a significant degree, either hinder or advance the therapeutic process. Monitor your growth as a professional therapist and as an individual by addressing the following questions periodically:

1. How do you feel when you hear someone describe the circumstances of their loss, especially if the scenes being described contain elements of violence or trauma?
2. Which losses are most difficult for you to hear about? In what ways do they remind you of your own losses or potential losses? What do you do with the feelings that are evoked when you are interacting with a grieving client?
3. How do you feel when you see a client cry uncontrollably? How do you respond?
4. What have you thought about your own death? How much personal reflection have you done in this area?
5. What work do you still need to do with regard to your own grief issues? What action have you taken that will enable you to do that work?

Assessing your issues surrounding dying and grieving is an emotionally difficult task, since it may awaken old feelings of loss that you thought you had effectively resolved. This task may be best undertaken in a group setting with other therapists asking similar questions of themselves, and with a trained helper who can offer support and guidance. As information enters awareness and insights are gleaned, it is usually accompanied by emotional intensity. Some of the authors' most powerful personal experiences have resulted from participating in structured group activities designed to elicit this kind of material. For information about experiential exercises, we suggest consulting *Thanatopics* (Knott, Ribar, Dudson, and King, 1989), which contains a wide range of thought-provoking activities related to grief and loss.

Your Motivation as a Helper

People decide to work in the field of counseling and therapy and in the specific area of grief and loss for many reasons. Because there are healthy as well as unhealthy motives for these choices, it is important that therapists understand their own motivations before undertaking direct work with clients. We will examine two motivational factors that can greatly affect your therapeutic work: your previous losses and your current psychological needs.

Your own losses

All therapists have their own losses with which they must cope. Your history of loss can either enhance the therapeutic process or impede it. Many people who practice grief and loss therapy do so because of a loss they themselves have had. Because of their own experience, they know it can be a turning point for individuals and families—for better or for worse. They also know the tremendous need for support that the bereaved have. In many cases, the therapist's personal experience will allow him or her to have greater empathy for clients and their families and a greater depth of understanding of what they are experiencing. But sometimes it can turn into a mutual support group if the therapist has not done his or her own grief work. The situation can become even more complicated when the therapist suffers a loss (which happens eventually to everyone) while also seeing others who are grieving. There are few guidelines in this regard, but we suggest that the therapist seek professional consultation to help judge his or her ability to do effective therapy at this time.

Psychological needs

Some professionals have difficulty separating their own needs from those of their clients. They may also be unable to differentiate between effective helping and enabling. The term *codependent* has been applied primarily to dysfunctional relationships and families, but we agree with Wolfelt (1991), who suggests that it can apply to therapists working with grief and loss as well. He describes the codependent bereavement caregiver as one who "often confuses caregiving with caretaking." A therapist who consistently puts the needs of clients before his or her own is in danger of burnout and may have fallen into the trap of codependency. This pattern may occur when the therapist has unresolved grief issues that he or she is indirectly trying to work out by working with the bereaved, or when the therapist's self-esteem comes exclusively from "fixing" others. The warning signs include (1) thinking of oneself as indispensable to clients, (2) constantly worrying about clients even when away from work, (3) neglecting one's own relationships, and (4) a tendency to overcommit (Wolfelt, 1991). None of us is immune to this condition, and it is for this reason that personal therapy and professional supervision are important elements in our continued development and self-awareness.

Learning to Set Limits

One of the most difficult tasks for grief therapists is deciding the size of client load they can handle, especially regarding grief-related cases. Many therapists see only a few bereaved individuals or families at any one time because of the demands this kind of work places on them. If you are a therapist in a hospice or cancer clinic, this may not be an option. In these settings, therapists may do education and outreach as part of their job, thus reducing the intensity of their work and providing some relief from the pain and sadness that accompanies grieving. The term *surrogate griever* has been used to refer to the role that professionals sometimes play in situations involving death. It is easy to get too caught up in the emotions of the client and be unable to maintain the distance necessary to do effective therapy.

Being a grief therapist also involves learning to combat burnout. One of us remembers well one year when she was teaching two university courses on death, dying, and grief; seeing clients in grief therapy; and writing a textbook on the subject. Toward the end of the spring, she was asked to speak on the topic of grief at a local conference. After her presentation, she went to hear another speaker who was discussing a case involving a mother whose two children had died in a tragic train accident. Sitting there, watching the intense grief of the mother on videotape, a voice inside proclaimed, "I cannot bear to hear about any more sadness and pain!" She listened carefully, got up, went home, and went for a long walk. She then spent a long weekend doing all her favorite things with her loved ones as a reminder of how much life is to be cherished. We suggest that you learn to pay close attention to your inner voice. It can be a very good friend.

How the Experience Will Change You

If you work in the area of grief and loss for very long, you will be changed in subtle and sometimes dramatic ways. One of us stopped practicing general psychotherapy after several years of doing grief therapy, realizing that while cognitively she could appreciate the struggles of all clients, emotionally, at some level, she was more invested in her work with bereaved families. Recognizing that these unconscious feelings could undermine the effectiveness of therapy, she chose to limit the focus of her practice and concentrate on the area in which she had the greatest commitment. The other author has found that his work with the bereaved, as well as his own experience with loss, has given him a renewed sense of spirituality and spawned an intense interest in the mind-body connection. This has manifested itself in his work with cancer patients as they strive to enhance their quality of life.

Practicing grief therapy makes you more keenly aware of the many personal tragedies that can and do occur. You can no longer tell yourself, "It can't happen to me." You know that it *can* happen to you. What comes with this realization, however, is a deep appreciation for life and living, and it is this that we hope to leave you with as we conclude this book. Exploring the realm of death and grief promotes an awareness of a more complex sense of reality than many of us are readily able to embrace. This reality involves the dynamic tension between one's unlimited possibilities for growth and one's ultimate finiteness. Reconciliation of these two forces means accepting life as a mandate to pursue your potential and expand your capacity as a human being.

References

American Association of Suicidology (1990). *Surviving suicide, 2* (2), Summer, 5.

American Psychiatric Association (1987). *Diagnostic and statistical manual of mental disorders* (3d ed.). Washington, DC: Author.

Aponte, H. J. (1990). Ethnicity dynamic important in therapeutic relationship. *Family Therapy News, 21*(5), 3.

Attig, T. (1986). Death themes in adolescent music: The classic years. In C. A. Corr and J. N. McNeil (Eds.), *Adolescence and death* (pp. 32–56). New York: Springer.

Aubrey, R. R. (1977). Adolescents and death. In E. R. Prichard, J. Collard, B. A. Drevitt, A. H. Kutscher, I. Seeland, and N. Lefkowitz (Eds.), *Social work and the dying patient and family* (pp. 131–45). New York: Columbia University Press.

Avort, A. van der, and Harberden, P. (1985). Helping self-help groups: A developing theory. *Psychotherapy, 22*(2), Summer, 269–72.

Balk, D. E. (1989). Arousing empathy and promoting prosocial behavior toward bereaved peers: Using guided fantasy with elementary school children. *Death Studies, 13*, 425–42.

——— (1991). Death and adolescent bereavement: Current research and future directions. *Journal of Adolescent Research, 6*(1), 7–27.

Bandura, A. (1969). *Principles of behavior modification.* New York: Holt, Rinehart and Winston.

Barett, T. W., and Scott, T. B. (1989). Development of the grief experience questionnaire. *Suicide and Life-Threatening Behavior, 19*(2), 201–15.

Beck, A., Rush, A., Shaw, B., and Emery, G. (1979). *Cognitive therapy of depression.* New York: Guilford Press.

Beck, A., Ward, C., Mendelson, M., Mock, J., and Erbaugh, J. (1961). An inventory for measuring depression. *Archives of General Psychiatry, 4,* 561–71.

Bell, N. K. (1989). AIDS and women: Remaining ethical issues. *AIDS Education and Prevention, 1,* 22–29.

Benoliel, J. Q. (1985). Loss and adaptation: Circumstances, contingencies, and consequences. *Death Studies, 9,* 217–33.

Berson, R. J. (1988). A bereavement group for college students. *Journal of Group Psychotherapy, Psychodrama and Sociometry, 41*(3), 101–17.

Bonanno, G. A. (1990). Remembering and psychotherapy. *Psychotherapy, 27*(2), 175–86.

Bourdon, L. S. (1991). *Grief and loss in survivors of sexual abuse.* Master's thesis, Colorado State University, Fort Collins.

Bowlby, J. (1969). *Attachment and loss.* New York: Basic Books.

——— (1973). *Separation.* New York: Basic Books.

——— (1980). *Loss: Sadness and separation.* New York: Basic Books.

Boyd-Franklin, N. (1989). *Black families in therapy: A multisystems approach.* New York: Guilford Press.

Bridges, W. (1980). *Transitions.* New York: Addison-Wesley.

Buell, J. S., and Bevis, J. (1989). Bereavement groups in the Hospice program. *Hospice Journal, 5*(1), 107–18.

Burnell, G. M., and Burnell, A. L. (1989). *Clinical management of bereavement.* New York: Human Sciences Press.

Busick, B. S. (1989). Grieving as a hero's journey. *Hospice Journal, 5*(1), 89–105.

Caine, L. (1988). *Being a widow.* New York: William Morrow.

Campbell, J. (1968). *The hero with a thousand faces.* Princeton: Princeton University Press.

——— (1971). *The portable Jung.* New York: Viking.

Centers for Disease Control (1989, August). *HIV/AIDS surveillance report.* Atlanta: U.S. Dept. of Health and Human Services.

Colgrove, M., Bloomfield, H., and McWilliams, P. (1983). *How to survive the loss of a love.* New York: Bantam Books.

Cook, A. S., and Oltjenbruns, K. A. (1982). A cognitive developmental approach to death education for adolescents. *Family Perspective, 16,* 9–14.

——— (1989). *Dying and grieving: Lifespan and family perspectives.* New York: Holt, Rinehart and Winston.

Corey, M. S., and Corey, G. (1987). *Group: Process and practice.* Monterey, CA: Brooks/Cole.

Cunningham, J. M., and Matthews, K. L. (1982). Impact of multiple-family therapy approach on a parallel latency-age/parent group. *International Journal of Group Psychotherapy, 32,* 91–102.

Davidsen-Nielsen, M., and Leick, N. (1988). Open group treatment model for acute, delayed and repressed grief reactions. In E. Chigier (Ed.), *Grief and bereavement in contemporary society*, Vol. 2 (pp. 83–87). London: Freund Publishing House.

Delgado, M. (1981). Hispanic cultural values: Implications for groups. *Small Group Behavior, 12*, 69–80.

Demi, A. S., and Miles, M. S. (1987). Parameters of normal grief: A Delphi study. *Death Studies, 11*(6), 397–412.

DiMaio, M., and Prunkl, I. (1986). The making of a youth grief support group. *Thanatos, 12*(4), 5–6.

Doka, K. J. (1989). *Disenfranchised grief: Recognizing hidden sorrow.* Lexington, MA: Lexington Books.

Dunn, R. G., and Morrish-Vidners, D. (1987). The psychological and social experience of suicide survivors. *Omega, 18*(3), 175–215.

Dunne, E. J., McIntosh, J. L., and Dunne-Maxim, K. (1987). *Suicide and its aftermath.* New York: W. W. Norton.

Eisenbruch, M. (1984). Cross-cultural aspects of bereavement. II: Ethnic and cultural variations in the development of bereavement practices. *Culture, Medicine and Psychiatry, 8*, 315–47.

Elde, C. (1986). The use of multiple group therapy in support groups for grieving families. *American Journal of Hospice Care, 3*(6), 27–31.

Falicov, C. J. (1982). Mexican families. In M. McGoldrick, J. K. Pearce, and J. Giordano (Eds.), *Ethnicity and family therapy* (pp. 134–63). New York: Guilford Press.

Faschingbauer, T. R., Zisook, S., and DeVaul, R. (1987). The Texas Revised Inventory of Grief. In S. Zisook (Ed.), *Biopsychosocial aspects of bereavement* (pp. 111–24). Washington, DC: American Psychiatric Press.

Figley, C., and Salison, S. (1980). Treating Vietnam veterans as survivors. *Evaluation and change: Services for survivors.* 135–41.

Folken, M. H. (1990). Moderating grief of widowed people in talk groups. *Death Studies, 14*, 171–76.

Freedheim, D. K., and Russ, S. R. (1983). Psychotherapy with children. In C. E. Walker and M. C. Roberts (Eds.), *Handbook of child clinical psychology* (pp. 978–94). New York: John Wiley and Sons.

Freud, S. (1917). Mourning and melancholia. In J. Strachey (Ed.), *The standard edition of the complete psychological works of Sigmund Freud*, Vol. 14 (pp. 243–58). London: Hogarth Press, 1957.

Frierson, R. L., Lippmann, S. B., and Johnson, J. (1987). AIDS: Psychological stress on the family. *Psychosomatics, 28*(2), 65–68.

Fritsch, J. (1988). *The anguish of loss.* Long Lake, MN: Wintergreen Press.

Fromm-Reichmann, F. (1950). *Principles of intensive psychotherapy.* Chicago: University of Chicago Press.

Gabriel, R. M., and Kirschling, J. M. (1989). Assessing grief among the bereaved elderly: A review of existing measures. *Hospice Journal, 5*(1), 29–54.

Gaines, A. D. (1986). Trauma: Cross-cultural issues. *Advances in Psychosomatic Medicine, 16,* 1–16.

Gaines, T., Jr. (1986). Applications of child group psychotherapy. In A. E. Riester and I. A. Kraft (Eds.), *Child group psychotherapy* (pp. 103–21). Madison, CT: International Universities Press.

Gardner, R. A. (1971). *Therapeutic communication with children: The mutual storytelling technique.* New York: Jason Aronson.

Gergen, M. M., and Gergen, K. J. (1984). The social construction of narrative accounts. In K. J. Gergen and M. M. Gergen (Eds.), *Historical social psychology* (pp. 173–89). Hillsdale, NJ: Lawrence Erlbaum.

Gilligan, C. (1982). *In a different voice.* Cambridge: Harvard University Press.

Gould, W. (1988). Seven unhealthy responses to bereavement. In E. Chigier (Ed.), *Grief and bereavement in contemporary society,* Vol. 1 (pp. 76–81). London: Freund Publishing House.

Granot, T. (1988). Group work with bereaved parents. In E. Chigier (Ed.), *Grief and bereavement in contemporary society,* Vol. 3 (pp. 124–30). London: Freund Publishing House.

Greif, G. L., and Porembski, E. (1988). AIDS and significant others: Findings from a preliminary exploration of needs. *Health and Social Work, 13*(4), 259–65.

Hall, C. W. (Ed.) (1980). *Psychiatric presentations of medical illness.* New York: Medical and Scientific Books.

Haran, J. (1988). Use of group work to help children cope with the violent death of a classmate. *Social Work in Groups, 11*(3), 79–92.

Hatton, C. L., and Valente, S. M. (1981). Bereavement group for parents who suffered a suicidal loss of a child. *Suicide and Life-Threatening Behavior, 11*(3), 141–50.

Ho, M. K. (1987). *Family therapy with ethnic minorities.* Newbury Park, CA: Sage Publications.

Hogan, N. S. (1987). *An investigation of the adolescent sibling bereavement process and adaptation.* Doctoral disseration, Loyola University, Chicago.

———— (1988). The effects of time on the adolescent sibling bereavement process. *Pediatric Nursing, 14,* 333–35.

Hogancamp, V., and Figley, C. (1983). War: Bringing the battle home. In C. Figley and H. McCubbin (Eds.), *Stress and the family: Coping with catastrophe,* Vol. 2 (pp. 148–65). New York: Brunner/Mazel.

Hudson, S., and Luke, S. (1988). Shared grief. In E. Chigier (Ed.), *Grief and bereavement in contemporary society,* Vol. 3 (pp. 143–46). London: Freund Publishing House.

Hynes, A. M., and Hynes-Berry, A. (1986). *Bibliotherapy: The interactive process.* Boulder, CO: Westview Press.

Ishii, S., and Bruneau, T. (1991). Silence and silences in cross-cultural perspective: Japan and the United States. In L. A. Samovar and R. E. Porter (Eds.),

Intercultural communication: A reader (6th ed.) (pp. 314–19). Belmont, CA: Wadsworth.

Jacobs, S. C. (1988). Bereavement and anxiety disorders. In E. Chigier (Ed.), *Grief and bereavement in contemporary society*, Vol. 1 (pp. 90–96). London: Freund Publishing House.

James, B. (1989). *Treating traumatized children: New insights and creative interventions.* Lexington, MA: Lexington Books.

Justice, B. (1988). *Who gets sick?* New York: St. Martin's Press.

Kalish, R. A., and Reynolds, D. K. (1976). *Death and ethnicity: A psychocultural study.* Los Angeles: University of Southern California Press.

Kamerman, J. B. (1988). *Death in the midst of life: Social and cultural influences on death, grief and mourning.* Englewood Cliffs, NJ: Prentice-Hall.

Kaplan, M. F. (1988). A peer support group for women in prison for the death of a child. *Journal of Offender Counseling, Services and Rehabilitation, 13*(1), 5–13.

Kastenbaum, R. J. (1969). Death and bereavement in later life. In A. H. Kutscher (Ed.), *Death and bereavement* (pp. 28–54). Springfield, IL: Charles C Thomas.

Klass, D. (1987). John Bowlby's model of grief and the problem of identification. *Omega, 18*(1), 13–32.

Klein, S. J., and Fletcher, W. (1986). Gay grief: An examination of its uniqueness brought to light by the AIDS crisis. *Journal of Psychosocial Oncology, 4*(3), Fall, 15–25.

Kleinman, A., Kaplan, B., and Weiss, R. (1984). Sociocultural influences. In M. Osterweis, F. Solomon, and M. Green (Eds.), *Bereavement: Reactions, consequences, and care* (pp. 199–212). Washington, DC: National Academy Press.

Knott, J. E. (1976). Resolving personal loss. In D. J. Drum and J. E. Knott (Eds.), *Structured groups for facilitating development* (pp. 78–86). New York: Human Sciences Press.

Knott, J. E., Ribar, M. C., Dudson, B. M., and King, M. R. (1989). *Thanatopics: Activities and exercises for confronting death.* Lexington, MA: Lexington Books.

Kollar, N. R. (1989). Rituals and the disenfranchised griever. In K. J. Doka (Ed.), *Disenfranchised grief: Recognizing hidden sorrow* (pp. 271–85). Lexington, MA: Lexington Books.

Koocher, G. P. (1983). Grief and loss in childhood. In C. E. Walker and M. C. Roberts (Eds.), *Handbook of clinical child psychology* (pp. 1273–84). New York: John Wiley and Sons.

Kübler-Ross, E. (1969). *On death and dying.* New York: Macmillan.

Kushner, H. (1981). *When bad things happen to good people.* New York: Avon Books.

Lagrand, L. E. (1986). *Coping with separation and loss as a young adult.* Springfield, IL: Charles C Thomas.

Land, H., and Harangody, G. (1980). A support group for partners of persons with AIDS. *Journal of Contemporary Human Services, 71*(8), 471–81.

Lattanzi, M. and Hale, M. E. (1984). Giving grief words: Writing during bereavement. *Omega, 15*(1), 45–52.

Lesee, S. (Ed.) (1983). *Masked depression.* New York: Jason Aronson.

LeShan, E. (1988). *Learning to say good-by: When a parent dies.* New York: Avon Books.

Levine, S. (1984). *Meetings at the edge.* Garden City, NY: Anchor Press.

Lewis, I. (Ed.) (1977). *Symbols and sentiments.* London: Academic Press.

Lewis, R. (1985). Cultural perspective on treatment modalities with Native Americans. In M. Bloom (Ed.), *Life-span development: Bases for preventive and interventive helping* (pp. 458–64). New York: Macmillan.

Lindemann, E. (1979). *Beyond grief: Studies in crisis intervention.* New York: Jason Aronson.

Lister, L. (1977). Cultural perspectives on death as viewed from within a skilled nursing facility. In E. R. Prichard et al. (Eds.), *Social work with the dying patient and family* (pp. 216–29). New York: Columbia University Press.

Lochner, C. W., and Stevenson, R. G. (1988). Music as a bridge to wholeness. *Death Studies, 12,* 173–80.

London, H., and Devore, W. (1988). Layers of understanding: Counseling ethnic minority families. *Family Relations, 37,* 310–14.

Lukas, C., and Seiden, H. (1987). *Silent grief: Living in the wake of suicide.* New York: Bantam Books.

MacLennan, B. W. (1986). Child group psychotherapy in special settings. In A. E. Riester and I. A. Kraft (Eds.), *Child group psychotherapy* (pp. 83–101). Madison, CT: International Universities Press.

Malinak, D. O., Hoyt, M. F., and Patterson, V. (1979). Adult's reactions to the death of a parent: A preliminary study. *American Journal of Psychiatry, 136*(9), 1152–56.

Marsella, A. J., and Pedersen, P. B. (Eds.) (1981). *Cross-cultural counseling and psychotherapy.* New York: Pergamon Press.

Martinez, C., Jr. (1988). Mexican-Americans. In L. Comas-Diaz and E. H. Griffith (Eds.), *Clinical guidelines in cross-cultural mental health* (pp. 182–201). New York: John Wiley and Sons.

Masterman, S. H., and Reams, R. (1988). Support groups for bereaved preschool and school-age children. *American Journal of Orthopsychiatry, 58*(4), 562–70.

Matsumoto, G. M., Meredith, G. M., and Masuda, M. (1970). Ethnic identity: Honolulu and Seattle Japanese-Americans. *Journal of Cross-Cultural Psychology, 1,* 63–76.

May, R. (1975). Values, myths, and symbols. *American Journal of Psychiatry, 132*(7), 703–6.

McCubbin, H., and Patterson, J. (1983). The family stress process: The double ABCX model of adjustment and adaptation. In H. I. McCubbin, M. Sussman, and J. Patterson (Eds.), *Social stress and the family: Advances and developments in family stress theory and research* (pp. 7–37). New York: Haworth Press.

McKinney, R. (1976). Free writing as therapy. *Psychotherapy: Theory, Research, and Practice, 13*(2), 183–86.

McGoldrick, M., and Rohrbaugh, M. (1987). Researching ethnic family stereotypes. *Family Process, 26,* 89–99.

Mills, J. C., and Crowley, R. J. (1986). *Therapeutic metaphors for children and the child within.* New York: Brunner/Mazel.

Minuchin, S. (1974). *Families and family therapy.* Cambridge: Harvard University Press.

Mishne, J. (1983). *Clinical work with children.* New York: Free Press.

Nachmias, S. (1988). The group technique as a means of social rehabilitation through self-help for widows. In E. Chigier (Ed.), *Grief and bereavement in contemporary society,* Vol. 3 (pp. 156–63). London: Freund Publishing House.

Neuberger, J. (1987). *Caring for dying people of different faiths.* London: Austen Cornish.

Nielson, M., and Leick, N. (1988). Open group treatment model for acute, delayed and repressed grief reactions. In E. Chigier (Ed.), *Grief and bereavement in contemporary society,* Vol. 2 (pp. 83–87). London: Freund Publishing House.

Ohlsen, M. (1977). *Group counseling.* New York: Holt, Rinehart and Winston.

Oltjenbruns, K. (1989). *Ethnicity and the grief response: Mexican-American and Anglo College Students.* Doctoral dissertation, University of Colorado, Boulder.

——— (1991). Positive outcomes of adolescents' experience with grief. *Journal of Adolescent Research, 6*(1), 43–53.

Osterweis, M., Solomon, F., and Green, M. (Eds.). (1984). *Bereavement: Reactions, consequences, and cure.* Washington, DC: National Academy Press.

Parkes, C. M. (1972). *Bereavement: Studies of grief in adult life.* New York: International Universities Press.

Parkes, C. M., and Weiss, R. S. (1983). *Recovery from bereavement.* New York: Basic Books.

Pelletier, K. R. (1977). *Mind as healer, mind as slayer.* New York: Dell Publishing.

Pincus, L. (1984). The process of mourning and grief. In E. Schneidman (Ed.), *Death: Current perspectives* (pp. 402–11). Palo Alto, CA: Mayfield Publishing.

Pirodsky, D. M. (1981). *Primer of clinical psychopharmacology: A practical guide.* New York: Medical Examination Publishing.

Potvin, L., Lasker, J, and Toedter, L. (1989). Measuring grief: A short version of the perinatal grief scale. *Journal of Psychopathology and Behavioral Assessment, 11*(1), 29–45.

Rando, T. A. (1984). *Grief, dying, and death.* Champaign, IL: Research Press.

——— (1985). Creating therapeutic rituals in the psychotherapy of the bereaved. *Psychotherapy, 22*(2), 236–40.

Raphael, B. (1983). *The anatomy of bereavement.* New York: Basic Books.

Raphael, B., and Nunn, K. (1988). Counseling the bereaved. *Journal of Social Issues, 44*(3), 191–206.

Rapoport, J. L., and Ismond, D. R. (1990). *DSM-III-R training guide for diagnosis of childhood disorders.* New York: Brunner/Mazel.

Reade, R. (1981). Harsh transition to a new way of death. *Social Work Today, 12*(41), 11–12.

Redburn, D. E., and Juretich, M. (1989). Some considerations for using widowed self-help group leaders. *Gerontology and Geriatrics Education, 9*(3), 89–98.

Reik, T. (1946). *Listening with the third ear.* New York: Arena Books.

Robinson, P. J., and Fleming, S. (1989). Differentiating grief and depression. *Hospice Journal, 5*(1), 77–89.

Rognlie, C. (1989). Perceived short- and long-term effects of bereavement support group participation at the Hospice of Petaluma. *Hospice Journal, 5*(2), 39–53.

Rosenblatt, P. C. (1988). Grief: The social context of private feelings. *Journal of Social Issues, 44*(3), 67–78.

Rosenblatt, P., and Elde, C. (1990). Shared reminiscence about a deceased parent. *Family Relations, 39,* 206–10.

Rubin, R. J. (1978). *Using bibliotherapy.* Phoenix, AZ: Oryx Press.

Rutter, M., Izard, C., and Read, P. (Eds.) (1986). *Depression in young people: Clinical and developmental perspectives.* New York: Guilford Press.

Saba, G. W., Karrer, B. M., and Hardy, K. V. (1989). Introduction to special issue on minorities and family therapy. *Journal of Psychotherapy and the Family, 6*(12), 1–15.

Salladay, S. A., and Royal, M. E. (1981). Children and death: Guidelines for grief work. *Child Psychiatry and Human Development, 11*(4), 203–12.

Samovar, L. A., and Porter, R. E. (Eds.) (1991). *Intercultural communication: A reader* (6th ed.). Belmont, CA: Wadsworth.

Sanders, C. M., Mauger, P. A., and Strong, P. N. (1985). *The grief experience inventory.* Palo Alto, CA: Consulting Psychologists Press.

Schaefer, C. E., and Reid, S. E. (1986). *Game play: Therapeutic uses of childhood games.* New York: John Wiley and Sons.

Schneider, J. M. (1980). Clinically significant differences between grief, pathological grief, and depression. *Patient Counselling and Health Education,* Fourth Quarter, 267–75.

Schoen, K., and Schindelman, E. (1989). AIDS and bereavement. *Journal of Gay and Lesbian Psychotherapy, 1*(2), 117–21.

Schwab, R. (1986). Support groups for the bereaved. *Journal for Specialists in Group Work, 11*(2), 100–6.

Shehan, C. L. (1987). Spouse support and Vietnam veteran's adjustment to post-traumatic stress disorder. *Family Relations, 36,* 55–60.

Siegel, K., Mesagno, F. P., and Christ, G. (1990). A prevention program for bereaved children. *American Journal of Orthopsychiatry, 60*(2), 168–75.

Silver, S. M., and Iacono, C. U. (1984). Factor-analytic support for DSM-III's post-traumatic stress disorder. *Journal of Clinical Psychology, 40*(1), 5–14.

182

Smith, C. A. (1989). *From wonder to wisdom.* Markham, Ontario: Penguin.

Spiegel, D. (1980). The recent literature: Self-help and mutual support groups. *Community Mental Health Review,* 5(1–4), 15–25.

Stearns, A. K. (1984). *Living through personal crisis.* New York: Ballantine Books.

Stillion, J. M., McDowell, E. E., and May, J. H. (1989). *Suicide across the lifespan—Premature exits.* New York: Hemisphere.

Sue, D. W., and Sue, D. (1990). *Counseling the culturally different* (2d ed.). New York: John Wiley and Sons.

Sugar, M. (1988). A preschooler in a disaster. *American Journal of Psychiatry,* 42(4), 619–29.

Tatelbaum, J. (1980). *The courage to grieve.* New York: Harper & Row.

Teyber, E. (1988). *Interpersonal process in psychotherapy: A guide for clinical training.* Chicago: Dorsey Press.

Tick, E. (1985). Vietnam grief: Psychotherapeutic and psychohistorical implications. In E. M. Stern (Ed.), *Psychotherapy and the grieving patient* (pp. 101–15). New York: Haworth Press.

Tigges, K. N., and Marcil, W. M. (1988). *Terminal and life-threatening illness.* Thorofare, NJ: Slack.

Vachon, M. L. S., and Stylianos, S. K. (1988). The role of social support in bereavement. *Journal of Social Issues,* 44(3), 175–90.

Vastola, J., Nierenberg, A., and Graham, E. (1986). The lost and found group: Group work with bereaved children. In A. Gitterman and L. Shulman (Eds.), *Mutual aid groups and the life cycle* (pp. 75–90). Itasca, IL: F. E. Peacock.

Vida, S., and Grizenko, N. (1989). DSM-III-R and the phenomenology of childhood bereavement. *Canadian Journal of Psychiatry,* 34, 148–55.

Volkan, V. D. (1981). *Linking objects and linking phenomena: A study of the forms, symptoms, metapsychology, and therapy of complicated mourning.* New York: International Universities Press.

Wachtel, E. F., and Wachtel, P. L. (1986). *Family dynamics in individual psychotherapy: A guide to clinical strategies.* New York: Guilford Press.

Walker, K. N., MacBride, A., and Vachon, M. L. S. (1977). Social support networks and the crisis of bereavement. *Social Science and Medicine, 11,* 35–41.

Walls, N., and Meyers, A. (1985). Outcome in group treatments for bereavement: Experimental results and recommendations for clinical practice. *International Journal of Mental Health,* 13(34), 126–47.

Walsh, R., and McGoldrick, M. (1988). Loss and the family life cycle. In C. J. Falicov (Ed.), *Family transitions: Continuity and change over the life cycle* (pp. 311–36). New York: Guilford Press.

Watzlawick, P., Weakland, J., and Fisch, R. (1974). *Change: Principles of problem formulation and problem resolution.* New York: W. W. Norton.

Weiss, R. (1974). The provisions of social relationships. In Z. Rubin (Ed.), *Doing unto others.* Englewood Cliffs, NJ: Prentice-Hall.

Weizman, S. G. (1989). Delayed and complicated grief: Psychotherapeutic methods of intervention. In E. Chigier (Ed.), *Grief and bereavement in contemporary society*, Vol. 2 (pp. 15–23). London: Freund Publishing House.

Weizman, S. G., and Kamm, P. (1985). *About mourning: Support and guidance for the bereaved.* New York: Human Sciences Press.

Westermeyer, J. (1987). Clinical considerations in cross-cultural diagnosis. *Hospital and Community Psychiatry, 38*(2), 160–65.

Wheeler, S. R., and Limbo, R. K. (1990). Blueprint for a perinatal bereavement support group. *Pediatric Nursing, 16*(4), 341–44.

Widdison, H. A., and Salisbury, H. G. (1990). The delayed stress syndrome: A pathological delayed grief reaction? *Omega, 20*(4), 293–306.

Wolfelt, A. D. (1987a). Resolution versus reconciliation: The importance of semantics. *Thanatos*, Winter, 10–13.

———— (1987b). Understanding common patterns of avoiding grief. *Thanatos*, Summer, 2–5.

———— (1988). *Death and grief: A guide for clergy.* Muncie, IN: Accelerated Development.

———— (1991). Exploring the topic of codependency in bereavement caregiving. *Forum Newsletter, Association of Death Education and Counseling, 15*(6), 7–8.

Worden, J. W. (1982). *Grief counseling and grief therapy.* New York: Springer.

———— (1991). *Grief counseling and therapy* (2d ed.). New York: Springer.

Wortman, C. B., and Silver, R. C. (1989). The myths of coping with loss. *Journal of Consulting and Clinical Psychology, 57*(3), 349–57.

Wrobleski, A. (1984). The suicide survivors grief group. *Omega, 15*(2), 173–85.

Yalom, I. D. (1975). *The theory and practice of group psychotherapy.* New York: Basic Books.

Yalom, I. D., and Vinogradov, S. (1988). Bereavement groups: Techniques and themes. *International Journal of Group Psychotherapy, 4*(38), October, 419–47.

Ybarra, S. (1991). Women and AIDS: Implications for counseling. *Journal of Counseling and Development, 69*(3), 285–87.

Zieman, G., Romano, P., Blanco, K., and Linnell, T. (1981). The process-observer in group therapy. *Group, 5*(4), 37–47.

Index

Index